MAHABHARAT

THE ETERNAL MIRROR OF HUMAN CONFLICT

K.N. SINGH

EDITED BY PRANITA LELE

BlueRose ONE.com
Stories Matter
NewDelhi • London

BLUEROSE PUBLISHERS
India | U.K.

For permissions requests or inquiries regarding this publication, please contact:

BLUEROSE PUBLISHERS
www.BlueRoseONE.com
info@bluerosepublishers.com
+91 8882 898 898
+4407342408967

ISBN: 978-93-7139-896-1

Typesetting: Pooja Sharma

First Edition: June 2025

ACKNOWLEDGMENT

This book has been a journey of reflection and revelation, and I owe its completion to the unwavering support and inspiration of those closest to me.

I extend my deepest gratitude to my family and friends, whose encouragement, insights, and affection have sustained me throughout this endeavor.

To my beloved wife, **Suman Singh**, for standing by me through every chapter of life—and every chapter of this book.

To my dear grandchildren—**Pranshuta, Urshita, Ishita, Hritwik, and Prajakta**—your curiosity, warmth, and thoughtful questions have deepened my reflections and inspired fresh insights.

To my four delightful great-grandchildren—**Sia, Viren, Ved, and Vayu**—you bring boundless energy, laughter, and a renewed zest for life. You remind me that while the *Mahabharat* speaks of ancient battles, the joy of the present is a victory in itself.

To my daughter, **Pranita Lele**, for your editing, which has helped shape and clarify my words while preserving the essence of my thoughts.

To my granddaughter, **Ishita**, who has once again designed the cover of this book. You have created the covers for all my books, and each one reflects your creativity, care, and deep understanding of my work.

And to every reader of this book—may it mirror not only the timeless conflicts of the *Mahabharat,* but also the enduring questions we each carry within.

With gratitude,

K.N. Singh

PREFACE

For centuries, many Indian households hesitated to keep the *Mahabharat* within their homes, fearing it brought discord. This caution perhaps reveals a deeper truth: the *Mahabharat* is not a mere story—it is a mirror. It reflects not only the grandeur of kingdoms and the valor of warriors but also our own internal conflicts, attachments, and failings. It disturbs because it awakens. It unsettles because it demands introspection.

Yet, beyond its unsettling truths, the *Mahabharat* also serves as a guide. Lord Krishna's counsel to Arjun is not confined to the battlefield; it transcends time. It teaches us to rise above personal attachments, to act with detachment, and to uphold justice—even when the path is bitter and strewn with loss. The wisdom of the Gita urges us to choose dharma over comfort, duty over despair.

This book seeks to reconsider a common simplification: that the war of Kurukshetra erupted solely because Duryodhan refused to return Indraprastha to the Pandavas. The roots of the conflict run far deeper. They lie in the inner landscapes of the characters—in their psychology, their choices, and the qualities that governed them. The epic intricately maps the interplay of the three gunas: **sattva** (purity, harmony), **rajas** (desire, restlessness), and **tamas** (ignorance, inertia). The Pandavas, striving towards sattvic ideals of restraint and divine wisdom, stood in contrast to the tamasic impulses of the Kauravas, marked by greed, pride, and hostility.

In the earliest times, humanity needed no king—people lived by dharma instinctively. But as desire, division, and ambition took root, leadership became necessary. The *Mahabharat* reminds us, however, that true leadership must rest on moral clarity and courage. Dhritarashtra, bound by his affection for his sons and blinded by self-love, failed not only as a father but as the sovereign of a vast empire. His inability to confront wrongdoing, even when truth stood before him, remains a cautionary tale for all forms of authority.

The story of Indraprastha, the kingdom granted to the Pandavas, stands as a symbol of rebirth and earned glory. From the desolate land of Khandavaprastha, the Pandavas carved out a city of vision, beauty, and strength—a triumph not of entitlement, but of effort. The Kauravas, despite privilege and power, failed to match this grace, consumed instead by envy and insecurity. This contrast—between inherited power and earned greatness—lies at the very heart of the epic.

Ultimately, the *Mahabharat* is not confined to ancient memory. It is a civilizational mirror. Its pages reflect the eternal cycles of ignorance and awakening, destruction and renewal. It invites us, the modern readers, to ask difficult questions: Are we, too, blind to justice when it threatens our own kin? Are we willing to speak up, or do we remain silent like Bhishma and Drona, watching adharma unfold?

To read the *Mahabharat* is to examine one's own ethical compass. It is not just a tale of war, but a journey through the human soul—a call to choose not comfort, but righteousness; not passive inheritance, but active virtue. Through this exploration, the book aims to delve into the behavioral and ethical voids in key characters of the epic, urging readers to examine the relevance of dharma in personal, social, and political life even today.

Let this not be merely an account of war, but a mirror—held up to power, pride, parenting, and human potential.

CONTENTS

CHAPTER 1

FROM CREATION TO CONFLICT: EARTH'S EVOLUTION AND MAN'S ETHICAL DEVOLUTION

"All knowledge has its origin in our perception." – Leonardo da Vinci

Creation Before Conflict: From Nebula to Narrative

Long before Dharma faltered and kingdoms bled, there was silence—a cosmic stillness before identity or ego. Around 14 billion years ago, in the heart of a swirling nebula, a burst of light shattered the void. A protostar was born, followed by planets forged in fire. One of them—Earth—blue, burning, and incomplete.

Creation, even then, carried the seed of conflict. Just as the Mahabharata begins with silence before the clarion of Kurukshetra, the universe too emerged from chaos—a mirror to the inner wars yet to come.

Even the Mahabharata begins with silence, a darkness before Dharma's light was questioned. In the womb of the universe, as in Hastinapur, creation and conflict were inevitable companions.

Earth Takes Shape: Water Before Wisdom

The Earth cooled, its crust cracked and ancient lava whispered of chilling under water. Zircon crystals, 4.4

billion years old, found in Western Australia, suggest that water existed even as Earth was still forming. Vapor condensed. Oceans were born in silence. In that water, the first whispers of life stirred—algae, unknowing, unfeeling. From the inorganic arose the organic, just as from Bhishma's vows arose a lineage—but without direction or inner evolution Like Hastinapur's warriors—physically powerful, spiritually empty—early life advanced without understanding its place in the web it spun.

Life's Enigma: Evolution Without Ethics

How did life emerge from lifelessness? Science still stumbles here. Proteins, essential for life, appeared inexplicably. Algae gave way to mollusks, then to fish, reptiles, birds, and eventually—humans. Movement evolved: swimming, crawling, flying, walking. But what of conscience? Moral consciousness did not evolve at the same pace.

The Mahabharat's world had the highest forms of intelligence, but not necessarily wisdom. The final product of evolution—man—did not inherit empathy, only ability. We built tools, not temperance. In Mahabharat's world, the clever thrived, but not always the good.

Myth and Memory: Avatars as Metaphors

The Vedas speak in symbols:

Matsya, the fish—life in water.

Kachhap, the tortoise—land and water.

Narasimha, half-beast, half-human—instinct in conflict with ethics.

Vamana, the dwarf—small in stature, but expansive in intent.

But in the Mahabharata, avatars remain symbolic. Men wore the guise of gods but fought like beasts. Transformation was external, not internal. Krishna's divine form is shown—yet only Arjun sees. The war follows anyway.

Shifting forms without values

Over billions of years, the Earth has reshaped itself—continents drifted, mountains rose, oceans receded. Life evolved alongside: fins became feet, instincts became intelligence. The *physical world* (land, earth) changes form constantly—through natural processes like erosion, earthquakes, and evolution—these changes are neutral, without value systems or ethics. Through all this transformation, conscience did not necessarily grow. Evolution was mechanical, not moral.

The Mahabharata reflects this same truth. Many characters undergo transformations—not just physical, but social or identity shifts: Karna, born a prince, raised as a charioteer's son, dies a hero—but his identity is always contested. Draupadi, a queen, is treated like a wagered object. Krishna, the divine, yet he plays the role of a diplomat, a charioteer, a strategist and counselor. These transformations in status, role, or appearance mirror evolution's ability to change form, but not always purpose. Just as biological evolution doesn't ensure ethical progress, neither does social or political change in the epic—or in our world. Progress in form doesn't mean progress in values. Despite divine presence and royal declarations, the war still happened. Righteousness was known, yet not followed.

In both nature and narrative, forms shift, but without the anchor of values, such change becomes a lie—a surface illusion. The Mahabharata teaches us that without dharma—ethical grounding—our progress is just motion, without any meaning.

Civilization Without Civility

By the Holocene epoch, humans walked great distances, settled near rivers, built homes and cities. Civilizations flourished. The Indus Valley was one such marvel—planned cities, uniform bricks, measured weights. Yet, beneath order lay inequality. Innovation bloomed; so did ambition. Even the most advanced civilizations did not guarantee ethical behaviour.

Just like Hastinapur—rich in scriptures, wise elders, and celestial weapons—still rotted from within. Greed, envy, deceit, and vengeance overshadowed greatness.

From Algae to Adharma

Excavations unearthed ancient lives—pottery, beads, fire altars. They spoke of ingenuity, yes, but also of impermanence. The final irony of evolution is this: though we've risen from algae to articulate beings, we still forget the simplest truths—kindness, restraint, humility.

And perhaps, this forgetting—this deliberate loss of noble intention—is what truly led to Kurukshetra.

Kurukshetra was not just a war between cousins. It was the eruption of conflicts: of ego, envy, silence, injustice. It is a mirror held up to all of us.

Because even after billions of years, and thousands of scriptures, the real battle remains unchanged— **Not in the skies. Not on the soil. But in the soul.**

CHAPTER 2

THE KINGDOM OF KURU AND THE DESCENT OF DHARMA

The Rise of Hastinapur

Long after the glory of the Indus Valley civilization had dimmed, newer kingdoms took root along the fertile plains of the Indo-Gangetic region. Stretching from the western Khandava forest to the eastern expanse of Pataliputra and beyond, this land saw the emergence of the powerful Kuru Kingdom, with its capital at Hastinapur. The Kurus were believed to be descendants of King Bharat, after whom the country itself was named. By 1200–800 BCE, Hastinapur had become a formidable political and cultural centre.

The Blind King and the Blindfolded Queen

Prince Dhritarashtra, born blind, ascended the throne not due to merit or vision, but by the traditions of primogeniture. He married Gandhari, a princess from Gandhar, who, aware of his blindness, chose to blindfold herself for life—an act lauded for its loyalty, but troubling in its symbolism. Gandhari's gesture, often romanticized, signified a deliberate refusal to witness and question the unfolding wrongs within her household.

Was it loyalty or silent compliance that let destruction brew unchecked?

Power Without Purpose

Dhritarashtra failed to embody the qualities expected of a king—courage, foresight, justice, and above all, moral clarity. Unlike rulers who ventured into forests for hunting, cultural patronage, or territorial conquests, he remained tethered to the throne, expanding not his influence but merely his lineage. Gandhari gave birth to one hundred sons and a daughter. His younger brother Pandu, despite having two wives—Kunti and Madri—fathered only five sons.

Kunti, one of the *Panch-Kanya,* held a different view: that quality, not quantity, defines strength. She voiced the wisdom that uncontrolled multiplication of heirs, without instilling restraint and ethics, leads to chaos.

Her foresight was tragically ignored.

When Lineage Breeds Lawlessness

The Kauravas, born into privilege, lacked the discipline of dharma. Their upbringing was marked not by humility or wisdom, but by entitlement and rivalry. Devoid of moral compass, they grew into schemers and deceivers, experts in manipulation—treating rules as obstacles to bypass, not principles to uphold.

The Pandavas, though fewer in number, were taught restraint, responsibility, and righteousness. Kunti had raised them to believe that family is a structure of support, not a battlefield of egos.

But such teachings withered in the hostile climate of Hastinapur.

The War of Broken Values

The Mahabharata was not just a war between cousins; it was a collision of intentions—between those who sought power at any cost, and those who tried, often imperfectly, to uphold dharma.

The Kuru Kingdom was a site of potential greatness, but it decayed under the weight of blind authority, suppressed conscience, and unchecked ambition. The collapse wasn't sudden—it was slow and silent.

It did not happen due to a single event. Instead, it unfolded gradually, through small, often unnoticed decisions where people chose silence instead of truth. They remained quiet when they should have spoken out against injustice. They chose lineage over integrity. They supported family or tradition even when it was morally wrong. They chose loyalty over justice. They stood by powerful figures not because they were right, but because of personal ties. The downfall of empires and values is often written not in one act of betrayal, but in the thousand small decisions to look away.

When kings are blind and queens choose not to see, kingdoms don't fall—they quietly decay from within.

CHAPTER 3

KANYA – THE WORSHIPPED YET WRONGED: A REFLECTION ON LOST INTENTIONS

Rituals That Remember What Society Forgets

In the grand narrative of the *Mahabharata,* we see gods descend, wisdom spoken, and dharma debated—yet time and again, noble behavior falters. Amid this chaos, one practice quietly persisted through the ages: *Kanya Puja*—the worship of young girls as manifestations of the divine. This ritual, though seemingly simple, carries profound intent. It reminds us of a value system in which purity, humility, and inner strength were revered—not just symbolically, but behaviorally.

Yet, the irony is stark: while *kanyas* were revered ritually, women in the epic were routinely wronged, dishonored, or used as political tools. *Kanya Puja,* then, becomes more than just a tradition—it becomes a cultural indictment.

From the Formless to the Feminine: Origins of Kanya Worship

In the earliest Vedic traditions, worship was directed toward *Avyakta*—the formless goddess. Over time, sages redirected this devotion into tangible form: the young, unmarried girl. This shift wasn't just symbolic. It was deeply intentional—a way of grounding reverence in lived human experience. In worshiping the *kanya,* society honored not just divine potential, but the values of gentleness, resilience, and purity she represented.

The practice continues today, especially during *Shardiya Navratri* and *Ram Navami,* when families invite at least five young girls, wash their feet, apply *roli* on their foreheads, perform *aarti,* offer meals, and give gifts. Yet few pause to reflect on its meaning. The act is meant not just to honor the girl, but to remind us that divinity resides in innocence—and society's first duty is to protect it.

The Five Kanyas: Purity Beyond Convention

The number five in *Kanya Puja* is deliberate, echoing the *Pancha Kanya* from the *Puranas*—**Ahilya, Kunti, Draupadi, Mandodari, and Tara**. These women were not perfect in a conventional sense, but they transcended their circumstances with grace and moral resilience. Despite marriages, hardships, and public scrutiny, they are considered *eternally pure*—not because they conformed, but because they endured without losing their inner light.

Their stories offer not just inspiration but introspection. When society fails them, it is they who uphold its spirit. Remembering them is believed to free one from sin, perhaps because their memory demands that we live more ethically ourselves.

Mahabharat's Women: Revered in Myth, Betrayed in Life

If Kanya Puja celebrates the divine feminine, the Mahabharat exposes how that divinity is often dismissed in life. Draupadi, born of fire, is humiliated in a court of kings and elders—none of whom rise to defend her dignity. Amba, a princess, is abducted by Bhishma and denied both her chosen love and her right to self-determination. Spurned, unheard, and broken, she reincarnates as Shikhandi, returning not as a victim but as a catalyst for Bhishma's downfall—fulfilling a vow that justice would not be denied forever. Kunti, torn between duty and motherhood, watches her sons destroy one another, her silence a shield and a wound. Gandhari, blindfolded in devotion to her husband, becomes a tragic witness to the ruin of her own lineage.

These are not just personal tragedies—they are societal failures. When the protectors become perpetrators or bystanders, reverence becomes hollow. The behavior seen in these pivotal moments lacks the very noble intention that rituals like Kanya Puja are meant to instill. The rituals that honour girls as goddesses ring hollow when real women are denied their voice, agency, and respect.

Tradition with a Message: The Philosophy of Offering First

The worship of kanyas during harvest seasons, like Navratri and Diwali, holds agricultural and ethical significance. Offering the first produce to the goddess—before any consumption—was a gesture of humility and gratitude. It symbolized restraint, a sense of collective belonging, and recognition that blessings are not to be hoarded, but shared.

The sage advice behind this tradition reflects behavioral dharma: the nobility of giving before receiving, of serving before demanding. In contrast, many key characters in the Mahabharat act from ego, entitlement, and desire—detached from this foundational ethic.

Cultural Transmission and the Journey of the Girl Child

The kanya is not only a symbol of divinity, but also of transition. Across cultures, a girl is raised in one home, only to move to another after marriage—carrying traditions, love, and values with her. This silent journey is the cultural thread that binds generations.

Take Draupadi, for example. She was born in the kingdom of Panchala and later came to live in Hastinapur, where she witnessed the fall of a great royal family. After the war, even though she lost all her sons, she still found the strength to comfort Dhritarashtra and Gandhari—the parents of the very people who wronged her. Instead of holding on to anger, she chose to bring peace. In her, we see the true meaning of 'kanya'—a woman who carries pain with grace, and stands with dignity even in the face of deep loss.

A Final Word: Honour in Action, Not Just in Ritual

The contradiction between worship and behavior is not just historical—it continues today. We perform Kanya Puja, but do we ensure the safety, education, and freedom of every girl? We revere goddesses, but do we honor the living?

The Mahabharat warns us: when noble behavior dies, rituals become shells. Let the worship of the kanya not remain a seasonal observance. Let it become a standard—a reminder to realign our intentions, our conduct, and our conscience.

The Mahabharat compels us to reflect:

Did the characters act out of righteousness, or self-preservation?

Did they worship the feminine, or merely use it as a metaphor?

And are we doing the same today?

The chapter of Kanya Puja is not just about reverence—it is about lost values, the erosion of behavior, and the disconnect between worship and action. Unless reverence transforms into respectful conduct, the spirit of this tradition will remain buried under layers of forgotten intent—just like so many ideals in the Mahabharat.

Let the Goddess Walk Among Us—And Be Safe.

CHAPTER 4

KUNTI – A LIFE SHAPED BY SILENCE AND SACRIFICE

A strong woman knows her strength for the journey, but a woman of strength knows it is the journey that will make her strong."

Kunti's life embodied this sentiment. Yet even her unwavering strength could not shield her from the consequences of a world where noble behaviour was often claimed, but rarely practiced.

Royal Birth, Rare Choice

Born as Pritha, the biological daughter of Shurasena and adopted by Kuntibhoj, Kunti came from the esteemed Yadava lineage. As Vasudeva's sister and Krishna's aunt, she stood at the crossroads of royalty and divinity.

Her swayamvar was an unusual moment of autonomy in a patriarchal world. She chose Pandu—not for his conquests, but seemingly for the righteousness he projected. Yet that very choice placed her in a marriage devoid of emotional foundation.

A Hasty Departure From Companionship

Barely had Kunti settled into the palace when Pandu left for military conquests. No dire threat prompted this urgency. It was a pursuit of glory, a quest for personal validation that left his young bride emotionally abandoned.

This behaviour—cloaked in duty but hollow at its core—echoes the Mahabharat's larger pattern: actions taken not with intent to uplift, but to assert, dominate, and escape.

When Sight Overpowers Sense

During his military expedition, Pandu encountered Madri of Madra—emerging from a pond, saree clinging to her frame. Desire flared, not devotion. His urge to possess her, rather than connect with her, led to a hasty second marriage.

Once again, behaviour triumphed over intent. He claimed a second wife under the guise of alliance and right—but the truth lay in fleeting attraction.

Sisterhood Sacrificed at the Altar of Pride

Madri's arrival brought not harmony but tension. Rather than extending warmth, she underlined differences—questioning Kunti's adoptive lineage, flaunting her own royal roots.

Kunti, however, chose dignity. She did not retaliate. She honoured her dharma, upholding the household's peace in the face of petty provocations. Her restraint, though noble, highlights the deeper problem: a world where women were left to mend what men broke. They were often expected to fix problems caused by others, especially the men around them.

A Curse Shaped by Misconduct

Pandu's impulsive hunting of mating deer—who turned out to be the sage Kindama and his wife in disguise—was yet another act done without reflection. The sage's curse was harsh: should Pandu ever approach a woman with desire, he would die.

This was not mere punishment; it was cosmic commentary. Pandu's behaviour lacked sanctity. Even nature retaliated against such disregard for the sacredness of union.

The Burden Kunti Bore

Kunti was more than a mother, more than a royal matriarch—she was a silent witness to a house collapsing under the weight of unchecked ambition and fragile pride. She did not spark the fires, yet she walked through them. Like many women today who navigate broken homes, carry unspoken grief, or parent through loss, Kunti bore the consequences of choices made by others—without ever having the power to choose herself.

Her strength was not in commanding armies or summoning curses. It was in staying upright in a world that constantly asked her to bend. In a story filled with warriors, kings, and gods, it is Kunti's quiet endurance that lingers. But let us be clear: her life was not a tribute to endurance—it was a question mark against a world that forced her to endure.

Reflections On Present-Day Parallels

Even in today's world, women continue to bear the fallout of reckless male choices. A heated argument turns violent, a bruised ego leads to abuse, a man's inability to handle rejection results in acid attacks or stalking. These are not far from the impulsive decisions that drove the Mahabharat's men—from Duryodhana's envy to Bhishma's vows that ignored women's agency. Hastinapur may be a kingdom of the past, but its mindset survives in courtrooms that question a woman's clothing, in families that silence daughters to preserve "honour," and in relationships where love is mistaken for control.

Why, in the Mahabharata, did men like Sage Kindama hold the power to curse, while women were denied such divine authority? Why were their voices missing in decisions that shaped destinies? The epic offers no direct answer—but in that silence lies a painful truth: power has long been a one-sided conversation.

Dharma Stands Only When She Stands Empowered.

CHAPTER 5

BOONS TURNED BURDENS

A Gift With Strings

Kunti was blessed by Sage Durvasa with a divine mantra—a secret power that could invoke any god to grant her a child without physical union. It was not just a boon but a divine trust, one that demanded restraint, maturity, and nobility of intent. Yet, driven by youthful curiosity rather than dharma or responsibility, Kunti invoked the Sun god. The result was Karna—born of divine radiance, but abandoned by the banks of the river due to social fear and shame.

This was not merely a lapse in personal judgment—it was a moral fracture. The act lacked the sacred intention such divine gifts demand. Instead of using the mantra with a sense of duty, Kunti's trial led to a lifetime of pain for her firstborn, who grew up without identity, status, or maternal love.

Sacred Births and Selective Memories

The Mahabharat is not alone in referencing miraculous births. King Dasharatha, longing for progeny, performed a sacred yagna. The fertility god emerged from fire, offering a divine pudding (payasam) to his queens, resulting in the birth of Rama and his brothers. Here, divine power met noble intention: the desire to continue dharma through lineage.

Similarly, Anjani bore Hanuman by the blessings of the Wind God. The Virgin Mary gave birth to Christ. These stories reflect the universe's mysterious ways—but they also underscore the purity of intent behind such miracles. Where intentions were righteous, the outcomes were transformative. Where intentions were self-serving, they bore the weight of karma.

Mantra and manifestation

A mantra is more than a string of syllables—it is energy condensed in sound. When recited with faith and discipline, it connects the seeker to the divine, turning the formless (nirakar) into form (sakar). Just as concentrated sun rays can ignite fire, mantras carry hidden force—subtle, sacred, and transformative.

But even fire, if misdirected, can destroy. The magic of reproduction, when stripped of reverence and dharma, becomes just another tool—misused, misapplied, and misunderstood.

Beyond the physical

Science studies what can be seen and measured. But mythology insists there is a greater unseen—forces that operate in the silence, in the dark soil before a seed sprouts, in the womb before life takes form. The mythological stories of miraculous birth are not just fables—they are metaphors urging us to understand creation as a sacred trust, not just a process to be hacked or hurried.

Science Behind the Script: Ancient Stories, Modern Mirrors

Some episodes in the Mahabharat—like Gandhari giving birth to a hundred sons, or Kunti invoking gods to bear children—may sound mythical. But today, science has found ways to explain and even replicate parts of these ancient stories.

For example, Gandhari's hundred sons, said to be grown from small pieces of flesh placed in pots, can be seen as an early idea of IVF (In-Vitro Fertilization)—growing life outside the human body. Similarly, Kunti's children, born through divine chants without physical contact, resemble assisted insemination by donors, a method used today in fertility treatments. These may be the first recorded cases of advanced reproductive techniques, long before science gave them names.

Modern medicine now uses frozen eggs, surrogate wombs, and hormonal treatments to help people have children—things that once existed only in myth. But the Mahabharat didn't just focus on the how of creating life—it also deeply considered the why. Every divine birth came with a purpose, responsibility, and moral consequence.

Today, while technology has advanced, the intent behind creating life often lacks the same depth of reflection. We can now choose when and how to bring children into the world—but do we also ask: Are we emotionally and ethically prepared to raise them?

The core question remains—are our intentions nobler today? In ancient times, divine processes were accompanied by ritual, prayer, and moral responsibility. In contrast, modern reproductive choices, while empowering, often bypass the emotional, psychological, and ethical readiness required to nurture life.

As Vidura, the wise advisor once told King Dhritarashtra:

"It is my duty to offer my counsel to you without fear or favor. It is for you to accept it or reject it."

Perhaps the Mahabharat still offers us such counsel—reminding us that science must walk hand in hand with wisdom.

In the Mahabharata, divinity did not fail—humanity did. The gods gave gifts, but it was man who tainted them with twisted intent.

CHAPTER 6

GLORIFICATION OF GOD OR MANIPULATION OF MIRACLES?

Divine Gifts, Human Desires

Actions done with the desire for fame, comfort, or recognition lose their sanctity. They may offer gains, but often of inferior worth and shallow intellect. In the Mahabharata, even divine interventions were not spared from the taint of human ambition.

Kunti, bound by circumstance and social stigma, invoked a sacred mantra to bear children, as her husband Pandu had been cursed with death should he engage in intimacy. At a time when childlessness was seen as a curse for women, her use of divine blessings wasn't rooted in personal ambition but in fulfilling dharma through progeny. Yet, the divine act was born out of compulsion—not celebration.

Sacred Intent or Social Pressure?

Ideally, marriage and childbirth are meant to continue the creative flow of life—not just to follow what society expects. In the Mahabharata, Kunti gave birth to Yudhishthira, Bhima, and Arjuna through divine blessings from the gods Yama, Vayu, and Indra. Though the births had a divine touch, the reasons were practical—linked to survival and social standing.

Madri, Pandu's second wife, felt jealous and wanted the same blessings. Although Madri had not treated

Kunti kindly, Kunti still helped her conceive twins—Nakula and Sahadeva—out of a sense of duty. It was a rare act of generosity in a time marked by jealousy and rivalry.

The Limits of Generosity

But human desire never gets fulfilled. Like Gandhari, Madri became focused on having more sons to gain power and prestige. When she wanted Pandu to ask Kunti for more help, Kunti refused—not out of ego, but on principle.

There was no looming population crisis in those days. Kunti's restraint came from a vision. She believed that having fewer children allowed parents to raise them with more love, better values, and stronger character. Her thinking was far ahead of her time—driven by wisdom.

When Devotion Becomes Ambition

Madri's longing for children was natural, but it signaled a deeper shift in intent. The gifts of God are sacred. But when manipulated for ego, competition, or social climbing, even miracles lose their meaning. What began as a sacred gift—the divine ability to bear children through celestial intervention—gradually turned into a tool for comparison and competition. The blessing of the God was no longer honoured for spiritual purpose; it became a way to gain influence, match status, and secure a stronger place in the royal household.

When Madri sought more children through Kunti's divine boon, it wasn't driven by devotion or duty—it was shaped by the pressure to keep up. Kunti's refusal was not an act of pride or resentment, but one of foresight. She understood that unchecked desire could dilute the meaning of sacred acts. Her restraint reflected wisdom, a deep awareness of when to stop. But to others, especially in a society obsessed with numbers and legacy, her decision seemed cold or selfish.

This is how power, even if not overtly misused, begins to lose its purity. And wisdom, instead of being valued, gets questioned—misunderstood in a world that begins to prize expansion over balance.

When miracles become tools and gods are summoned for personal gain, the divine does not vanish—but the dignity of devotion surely does

CHAPTER 7

INVITING SELF-DESTRUCTION

Desire Over Dharma

Madri, the younger wife of Pandu, drew him with the power of physical attraction. Though Pandu deeply loved Kunti, his attachment to Madri became overwhelming—more lust than love. Her beauty stirred in him a powerful desire that ultimately blinded his judgment.

Pandu, once wise and restrained, forgot the curse placed upon him by the Rishi—should he ever engage in physical union, it would lead to death. Overpowered by emotion and desire, he succumbed to temptation, leading to his tragic end. Lust, once unleashed, becomes a hunger that clouds reason and overpowers intellect.

A Moment of Truth and Farewell

Pandu's death struck like lightning in the quiet mountains where they lived in exile. As the funeral pyre was prepared, Kunti—bound by *stree dharma*—expressed her wish to perform *sati,* to follow her husband in death. But Madri intervened.

Consumed by guilt and grief, Madri claimed responsibility for Pandu's death. She saw herself as the reason his desire had led to destruction and insisted that she would immolate herself with him. In that final hour, despite her complicated feelings toward Kunti, she acknowledged Kunti's unmatched grace and requested her to raise her twin sons, Nakula and Sahadeva.

The Heart That Gave Without Asking

Kunti, though unloved by Madri and often mistreated, had earlier helped her bear children without being asked—purely out of duty and compassion. That same selflessness now echoed in Madri's dying request. Kunti did not hesitate. She accepted the responsibility with the warmth and resolve only a noble heart can offer. It was a reminder that behavioral excellence lies not in ritual or power—but in how we treat others, even those who may not treat us well in return.

Impulse Destroys; Responsibility Endures

Pandu's death was not simply the result of a curse—it was the outcome of desire overpowering wisdom. In today's world, this is echoed in choices where people ignore their inner compass for the sake of fleeting gratification—whether through infidelity, addiction, or reckless decisions that fracture families and futures. These actions, like Pandu's, may feel justified in the moment but often lead to irreversible consequences.

When Madri chose to end her life, Kunti did not see herself as burdened by having to raise Nakula and Sahadeva. She embraced them with the same care and commitment as her own. This reflects a timeless truth: while some surrender in the face of crisis, others quietly rise to the occasion. In the modern context,

Kunti's role parallels those who take responsibility without resentment—stepmothers, guardians, or caregivers—who choose compassion over complaint. Her strength lay in preserving unity, not claiming credit. In a world shaken by impulse, it is such silent endurance that holds families—and society—together.

It was not the curse that killed Pandu, but the conquest of desire over wisdom.

The Mahabharata does not merely recount fate or divine will—it reveals how the absence of noble intent and behavioral restraint led even the mightiest to self-destruction

CHAPTER 8

PALACE PEDAGOGY; WHEN LEARNING LOST ITS SOUL

Ashrams: A Model of Equality and Learning

In ancient India, the ashrams of rishis served as powerful institutions for mental, spiritual, and character development. Princes were sent not to places of comfort, but to the forests of wisdom. These gurukuls did not discriminate between royal blood and humble birth—Lord Krishna and Sudama studied side by side, sleeping under the same roof, sharing the same hardships. They learnt not just from the scriptures, but from life itself. The gurukul system was not based on wealth or status, but on the strength of one's will and the commitment to learning.

This environment was free from the concept of privilege. The emphasis was not on lineage or material wealth, but on character, self-restraint, and discipline. The teachers did not care for the student's social background, but focused on building virtues that would shape a strong individual. The first lessons were about cultivating patience, humility, and focus before ever wielding a weapon or learning deep knowledge.

The life in the gurukul was simple and austere, demanding both physical and mental strength. Students engaged in daily physical labor, worship, and meditation to build their bodies, minds, and spirits.

The aim was not just to prepare them for the battlefield but for the internal battles every person must face—such as conquering desires, overcoming weaknesses, and developing self-control. These disciplines were seen as the foundation for true leadership, not just power or knowledge. In this way, the gurukul was a place where students learned to forge inner strength, alongside their academic and martial skills, preparing them for both external and internal wars.

Discipline Over Comfort

Life in these ashrams was far from easy. From the moment the sun rose, young minds were engaged in prayer, meditation, martial training, social learning, and spiritual discipline. They learned the ways of dharma, self-sufficiency, and societal responsibility. These formative years moulded their conscience before their skills—ensuring strength of character before strength of arm.

A Shift from Gurukul to Palace

During the Mahabharata era, however, this ancient practice began to erode. Royal children, including the Pandavas and Kauravas, did not step into the forests. They were schooled within the palace walls, under the tutelage of Dronacharya. He was appointed by Bhishma due to his unmatched martial prowess and arsenal gifted by Parashurama—including divine weapons like Brahmastra, Narayanastra, and Vajra—Dronacharya became the royal preceptor, counselor, and resident warrior.

Favouritism Within the Walls

Dronacharya was a revered teacher of warfare, entrusted with shaping the future warriors of Hastinapur. Yet despite his role as a guru—expected to be fair, detached, and impartial—he became entangled in the politics of the palace. His allegiance leaned subtly but clearly towards the Kauravas, partly because he served under their father, King Dhritarashtra. As a royal subject, his loyalty often clouded his judgment, leading to visible differences in how he treated his students.

Although he trained all the princes, it was the Pandavas—especially Arjun—who approached the training with discipline, humility, and respect. The sincerity of the Pandavas reflected the values Kunti had instilled in them from a young age. Yet Dronacharya's favoritism—whether deliberate or unconscious—created an atmosphere of bias. This was dangerous in a space that was meant to nurture character, not competition.

A true teacher must rise above personal preferences and political influences. In the gurukul, where ideals of fairness and dharma should reign, even subtle partiality can distort a disciple's growth and create seeds of resentment. Dronacharya's imbalance may not have seemed severe at the time, but it mirrored the larger decay in Hastinapur—a kingdom where power often overruled principle, and where even the sacred bond between guru and shishya (teacher and student) began to fray under pressure.

Lack of Moral Foundation

The Pandavas, under the influence of their mother Kunti's early lessons in humility and duty, managed to retain their values despite the uneven playing field. The Kauravas, however, never received moral grounding—neither from their parents nor from their mentor. They learned warfare without purpose, knowledge without conscience. Their learning lacked the soul that binds knowledge to wisdom. Duryodhana mastered the mace, Ashwatthama the sword, others learned divine weapons—but none of this could redeem the absence of noble intent. Their minds were sharp, but their hearts remained clouded.

Skill without Conscience

Each prince became a master in some form of warfare. But the teachings lacked cohesion, and the palace environment encouraged competition, not character. Duryodhana's arrogance, Karna's insecurity, and Ashwathama's vengeance were not born out of poor education, but out of education that forgot its soul.

The gurukul system had once aimed to build a society of wise warriors. But in Hastinapur, it became an assembly line of skillful yet directionless individuals. The intent to empower was lost; only the power remained.

The education was complete, the warriors were trained—but the soul of the learning was compromised. Instead of nurturing unity, the palace fanned rivalry. A true gurukul instills humility alongside strength. What emerged from Dronacharya's training ground were not balanced warriors, but divided brothers—skilled in battle, but broken in trust.

Connecting Palace Pedagogy to the Present Day

The chapter *Palace Pedagogy; When Learning Lost Its Soul* serves as a mirror to modern education systems that often prioritize skill acquisition over value-based learning. Just as the royal children in the Mahabharata were trained in warfare and strategy within palace walls—devoid of the grounding influence of moral discipline—today's elite institutions sometimes churn out individuals rich in technical knowledge but lacking in emotional intelligence, empathy, or ethical grounding. The shift from ashram-style holistic nurturing to compartmentalized, performance-driven pedagogy echoes in modern classrooms where grades often overshadow character, and ambition outpaces integrity. When learning becomes a means to outshine rather than uplift, the soul of education—rooted in humility, curiosity, and compassion—is quietly lost.

It wasn't the lack of knowledge that destroyed the Kauravas—it was the absence of virtue in how that knowledge was used. When learning loses its soul, kingdoms lose their future.

CHAPTER 9

ROOTS OF CHARACTER: PARENTING THAT SHAPES DESTINY

The Silent Architects of Behaviour

Before any teacher or school shapes a child, it is the parents who play the most important role in building their character. From the earliest years, children watch, learn, and absorb everything from their mother and father—not just words, but actions, habits, and reactions. This influence is not limited to physical care; it is emotional, moral, and deeply spiritual.

Parents are the silent architects of a child's behaviour. Through everyday interactions—how they speak to others, handle stress, show kindness, or set boundaries—they teach children what is right and wrong. Values like honesty, patience, respect, and empathy are not taught in one lesson—they are picked up slowly, through consistent example.

Even before a guru or school enters the picture, it is the parents who plant the first seeds of discipline, self-control, and compassion. If these seeds are watered with love, fairness, and consistency, they grow into strong roots that shape a child's personality for life. The foundation laid at home decides how a child responds to the world—whether with anger or understanding, selfishness or service, pride or humility. In this way, parents are not just caregivers—they are the first and most lasting teachers in a child's life.

Two Mothers, Two Worlds

Gandhari and Kunti, wives to King Dhritarashtra and Pandu respectively, stood as stark contrasts in maternal foresight and emotional engagement. Gandhari bore a hundred children to satisfy her blind husband's desire for power and legacy. But in doing so, she lost the opportunity to nurture each child meaningfully. The result was a generation that lacked moral grounding, easily swayed by jealousy and hate.

Kunti, on the other hand, despite personal trials—including a life without the companionship of her husband Pandu—chose to raise her five sons with unwavering strength, restraint, and spiritual insight. She taught them to lead with dignity, to uphold dharma, and to balance personal desire with the larger good. Her sons—Yudhishthira, Bhima, Arjuna, Nakula, and Sahadeva—reflected her resolve and calm moral clarity.

Dhritarashtra: The Blindness beyond Eyesight

Dhritarashtra's physical blindness was symbolic of his deeper flaws—his refusal to see the truth, his indulgence of his sons' misdeeds, and his inability to make righteous decisions. As a father and as a king, he failed to instill a sense of right and wrong. Instead of guiding his sons toward nobility, he silently allowed their envy and ambition to grow unchecked. The

Mahabharata is not kind to him—not for his inability to see, but for his refusal to act when it mattered most.

Kunti's Silent Strength

Kunti's struggles were internal, silent, and often invisible. She carried pain without protest, sorrow without complaint. Yet she never allowed that suffering to infect her sons with bitterness. She raised them on the ideals of self-restraint, humility, unity, and wisdom. Her power did not lie in her physical might, but in her mental resilience and her moral teachings.

Modern Reflections: From Palaces to Parenting Today

Parenting today, just like in the royal household of Hastinapur, often struggles to balance love with discipline, and ambition with values. In the Mahabharata, Dhritarashtra's blindness was not just physical—it symbolized his emotional and moral inability to see his sons' faults. His love for Duryodhana turned into indulgence, and his silence in the face of wrongdoing led to disaster. Gandhari, though wise and aware, chose to blindfold herself—not just in solidarity, but also in silence—failing to correct the path of her sons.

In many modern homes, a similar pattern plays out. Parents, in the name of love, often turn a blind eye to their children's mistakes. Some overprotect, while others overindulge—chasing success, marks, or prestige, but forgetting to build values like humility, empathy, and responsibility. On the other hand, like Kunti, some parents focus on shaping character through early discipline and emotional grounding, even in difficult circumstances.

Today's children may have access to the best education, technology, and comforts. But without a strong moral foundation, they are vulnerable to the same dangers the Mahabharata warns us about—entitlement, arrogance, and ethical confusion. Dhritarashtra and Kunti are more than just ancient figures; they represent two parenting approaches—one that feeds ego, and another that nurtures integrity. The choice between them remains just as relevant in today's homes.

Parenting is not merely where a child's journey begins—it's the blueprint that shapes their destiny

CHAPTER 10

WHEN GURUS FAIL, GENERATIONS FALL

The Tarnished Halo Of Hastinapur's Guru

In the grand palace of Hastinapur, where princes were trained to uphold dharma, lived a teacher whose brilliance was unmatched—yet whose heart bore stains of pride, vengeance, and bias. Dronacharya, revered as the royal guru, was a master of weaponry and divine knowledge. But beneath his wisdom lay personal grudges and caste prejudice that cast a long shadow over his legacy.

Arjun once saved Drona from a fatal accident, earning his special favour and the sacred Brahmastra mantra. Drona praised him as the greatest archer. But this favouritism was not based purely on merit—it was also rooted in loyalty to the royal family and a desire to settle personal scores. He later sent his students to attack King Drupad, not to defend the kingdom, but to avenge an old insult—turning the idea of *guru-dakshina* into a tool of revenge rather than a lesson in righteousness. What kind of pedagogy teaches retaliation as a virtue? Dronacharya's order to attack Drupad was an abuse of power and a betrayal of his role as a teacher. Rather than rise above his past humiliation, he used his students as pawns in a vendetta, mirroring the behavior of present-day gang lords who use proxies to settle scores.

Nowhere is Drona's bias more visible than in the story of Eklavya. A young boy from the Nishada tribe, Eklavya carved a statue of Drona and self-trained with unmatched dedication. When Drona learned of his skill, he did not reward him—instead, he demanded Eklavya's right thumb as *guru-dakshina,* disabling him for life. His reason? Eklavya, being from a lower caste, was not fit to become a warrior of Hastinapur.

Drona's refusal to teach Eklavya might reflect the social norms of the time—but demanding his thumb, despite never having taught him, was unjust. It wasn't just about protecting Arjuna's position; it was about denying a capable student his future based solely on birth.

In both Arjun and Eklavya's stories, we see how Drona's personal loyalties and caste prejudice distorted the very principles he was meant to uphold. His actions remind us that wisdom without fairness can easily become a weapon of injustice.

A Silent Witness to Injustice

During the most horrific moment in the Kuru court—Draupadi's disrobing—Dronacharya remained a mute spectator. He did not rise in protest, nor did he guide his students toward righteousness. Instead, he watched silently, his silence becoming an accomplice to crime. Later, he chose to fight on the side of the Kauravas, abandoning the neutral wisdom expected from a guru of both warring sides. His loyalty to the throne overruled his loyalty to truth.

The Prejudice of Power

Dronacharya had all the powers of a seer, yet he failed to conquer the most basic flaw—a prejudiced mind. His decisions were guided by resentment, favoritism, and social hierarchy. A true guru is expected to lead with renunciation and unwavering ethical clarity. Drona possessed divine knowledge but lacked the inner renunciation that makes one worthy of being called a guru.

Modern-Day Parallel: When Mentors Misguide

In today's world, teachers, coaches, and mentors hold immense power to shape minds—but when that power is misused, the damage can be deep and lasting.

For example, a schoolteacher who favours high-performing students while ignoring those who struggle sends a clear message: worth is tied to marks, not effort or potential. This can demoralize students and kill their confidence.

A sports coach who focuses only on students from influential families, offering them more playtime or better training, mirrors the same unfairness Dronacharya showed. Talent is overshadowed by bias, and true merit goes unnoticed.

In universities or coaching institutes, we also find mentors who push students toward careers that serve the mentor's reputation, not the student's passion—forcing them into fields they do not love, all for external validation.

Sometimes, even spiritual or motivational leaders influence followers for personal fame, discouraging independent thought in the name of loyalty. Like Drona demanding obedience from his students to settle his personal grudge, these mentors use guidance as a tool of control.

When mentors forget that their primary role is to uplift and guide ethically—not to control, compete, or project their own frustrations—they do more than fail one student. They set a faulty example that ripples through society.

A true teacher doesn't just build skills, they build character. And when that responsibility is betrayed, it becomes a misuse of trust, not just of power.

The echo of the guru's silence does not just fail his students—it trains a generation in the art of submission, and selective morality.

CHAPTER 11

THE UNEXPECTED GIFT OF HOPE

The Birth of a New Hope

King Drupad, having lost half of his kingdom to Dronacharya, was consumed by grief and a burning desire for retribution. His mind fixated on having a son who could avenge the humiliation he had suffered. To fulfill this wish, he sought the blessings of the sages Yala and Upyaja, requesting them to perform a 'yagna' (ritual sacrifice) to grant him a son capable of exacting revenge on Dronacharya. However, when the ritual was completed, and his wife, Prishali, was asked to partake in the offerings, a delay in her return angered the sages. In their impatience, they poured the sacrificial offerings into the sacred fire, leading to a miraculous event: two children, a son and a daughter, emerged from the flames.

Although Drupad had hoped for a son to exact vengeance, fate granted him a beautiful daughter, Draupadi, along with her brother, Dhrishtadyumna. While Draupadi's birth was seen as a symbol of hope, it also marked the beginning of an unexpected path for Drupad—one that would lead him away from vengeance and toward a destiny he had never envisioned.

A Daughter of Sacred Fire

Draupadi was no ordinary child; she was born of fire, a divine creation of the yagna, making her known as Yagnaseni. The scriptures called her one of the five maidens, Panchkanya, whose name could purify the world of sins. While the kingdom rejoiced at the arrival of the twins, Draupadi carried not just her parents' hopes but also their unspoken desires. Her birth transformed the course of Drupad's life in a way he had not anticipated. His wish for a son and revenge now gave way to the arrival of a daughter whose fate was far greater than he could have imagined.

The Unsteady Mind and Unrealistic Expectations

Drupad's obsession with revenge against Dronacharya came from a restless, unbalanced mind. He was fixated on a singular goal—restoring his honor by taking down Dronacharya. Instead of letting go or finding peace, he became consumed by the need to restore his pride. This narrow focus blinded him to other possibilities. When he performed a yagna (sacrifice) to have a son who could defeat Drona, he unexpectedly received a daughter as well—Draupadi. But he failed to recognize this gift. His fixation on revenge made him overlook that life often offers something better than what we ask for, if only we are willing to see it. These gifts may not align with our expectations but are, in fact, the very things we need for growth and healing.

Modern Reflections: When the Mind Is Obsessed

In today's world, we too are often driven by unrealistic desires—whether it's the pursuit of success, perfection, or the need to take revenge. Like Drupad, we may become fixated on a particular outcome, unable to see that life has its own course. Our minds, like his, are often unsteady and dominated by emotions and external pressures, leading us to miss out on unexpected gifts and opportunities.

A student obsessed with becoming a doctor or engineer may ignore their true talents in art, writing, or business, pushing themselves into burnout. A professional fixated on revenge against a colleague may lose valuable time, energy, and peace instead of growing from the experience.

Parents who chase only academic marks in their children may miss the child's need for emotional support or creativity.

Sometimes, the most profound lessons come from the things we least expect, and only when we open ourselves to these surprises can we truly begin to understand our purpose.

When our minds become emotionally charged and unsteady—driven by comparison, revenge, or rigid goals, we lose the ability to adapt, reflect, and grow. Like Drupad, we may ignore life's unexpected blessings just because they don't match our plans. Real wisdom lies in staying emotionally balanced and open to the possibility that what we get may be better than what we wished for.

We fail to see that the greatest gifts often come in unexpected forms. Draupadi, born from fire, was the hope Drupad never asked for, but the salvation he so desperately needed.

CHAPTER 12

THE ILLUSION OF CHOICE

The Swayamvar That Changed It All: A Test of Focus and Reflection

Draupadi, the radiant princess of Panchala, was the very embodiment of beauty, grace, and mystique. With lotus-like eyes, copper-hued nails, and cascading curls, she was incomparable. So mesmerizing was her presence that every other woman seemed ordinary in comparison. Her father, King Drupad, sought to find a worthy husband for her through a Swayamvar—an ancient ceremony allowing a princess to choose her groom from among eligible suitors.

But this was no ordinary gathering. The test set forth was one of skill, not lineage or wealth. A golden fish revolved high above, while a bowl of still water beneath reflected its image. The task? To pierce the eye of the fish by looking only at its reflection. Warriors from across kingdoms—strong, wise, and power-hungry—assembled, many driven more by ego and desire than discipline. They failed, one by one, unable to harness the single-pointed concentration required.

It was Arjun who triumphed. With focused mind and steady hand, he pierced the fish's eye, winning Draupadi. Yet, this was only the beginning of a tale where choices were blurred, intentions were compromised, and destiny, not character, dictated outcomes.

When Obedience Spoke Louder Than Consent

Drupad, despite his earlier humiliation by Arjun under Dronacharya's command, welcomed him as a son-in-law. The victory was both personal and political. However, joy turned to confusion when the Pandavas returned home. Arjun, eager to surprise his mother, called out to her, "Look what I've brought!" Without looking, Kunti casually responded, "Share it equally among yourselves."

Bound by the sanctity of their mother's word, the five brothers decided to marry Draupadi collectively. She became the wife of all five Pandavas, spending a year with each brother in turn.

Draupadi did not protest. The woman who once watched the world's greatest warriors fail to win her hand now became subject to a more complex challenge – silently accepting a role assigned by others' words and others' will. Her silence wasn't acceptance – it was surrender. A result of loyalty to family, respect for elders, and the heavy weight of duty. From one man's victory sprang five bindings – but no one thought to ask the woman what she truly wanted.

A Prayer Granted in Five Forms

There is another version of Draupadi's story, told in spiritual tradition. As a young girl, she prayed with great devotion to Lord Shiva. Her prayer was sincere and specific: she wished for a husband who would be strong, wise, handsome, righteous, and skilled in warfare. Lord Shiva, moved by her devotion, appeared before her but gently pointed out a truth—no single mortal man could embody all these virtues. But because her prayer was so sincere, he blessed her with five husbands in her next life—each one holding one of the qualities she longed for.

Thus, Draupadi's prayer was not denied, but fulfilled in a form no one—perhaps not even she—had imagined. She was destined to marry the five Pandavas, each representing one part of her ideal. Her fate, then, was not a mistake or misstep, but a divine orchestration—a prayer granted in five forms. Sometimes, what feels like fate or burden may actually be the unfolding of a deeper wish we once made.

Modern-Day Reflection: From Hastinapur to Himalayan Hamlets

The story of Draupadi, bound to five husbands, finds a curious echo in the Himalayan regions of Jaunswar Bawar and Kinnaur regions of Himachal where polyandry is still practiced—not as a spiritual destiny, but as an economic necessity. In this mountainous terrain, where arable land is scarce and survival hangs by a thread, families avoid dividing property by having all brothers share a single wife. The tradition, rooted in practical survival, mirrors the symbolic tale of Draupadi—where sharing was ordained not by choice, but by obligation.

Here, women called *rantys* live with multiple husbands, expected to show equal affection to each, though emotional preference and tensions often emerge. Women who leave these unions become *dhyantys,* returning to their parental homes with the rare agency to remarry—but only if the new husbands can afford to pay off the former ones. In both the epic and the present, the woman becomes a shared solution to a larger social issue—whether it's upholding dharma, managing inheritance, or preserving land.

This parallel forces us to reflect on how often women's lives are shaped by the weight of circumstances—be it myth, tradition, or survival. Whether in the palaces of Hastinapur or the remote valleys of the Himalayas, the question remains the same: how often do women get to choose, when the world around them keeps deciding for them?

From palace halls to mountain hamlets, the tale remains unchanged—when survival, tradition, or pride take the lead, a woman's choice is the first to be sacrificed.

CHAPTER 13

THE DICE GAME: WHEN STRATEGY KILLED SANCTITY

The Invitation That Was a Trap

Duryodhan invited the Pandavas and Draupadi to Hastinapur for a game of dice. It seemed like a friendly match, but the real plan was to trick the Pandavas and take everything they owned. Duryodhan, guided by his shrewd uncle Shakuni and supported by Karna, had no intention of playing fair. They had one goal—to strip the Pandavas of all they owned, piece by piece, until not even their dignity remained.

More Than Just a Game

Dice games, in their innocent form, are mere amusement. But once stakes—be they wealth, land, or people—enter the equation, it mutates into something far more sinister: a gamble with destiny. Yudhishthir, who believed in honesty and fairness, didn't realize that this game was full of hidden traps. His optimism blinded him to the malice behind the invitation. The dice, etched with numbers 1 through 6, became tools not of chance but of manipulation in the hands of Shakuni, a master of illusion and deceit.

A Game of Greed, Not Sport

Yudhishthir lost everything—his kingdom, his wealth, his brothers' freedom—and yet, he played on. Hope can be a virtue, but in the wrong hands, it becomes a weapon. When all was gone, he staked Draupadi—no longer a player but a pawn in a game that was never fair. The loss wasn't just material; it was moral, exposing a chilling void where values once lived.

A Mirror to Modern Morality

This tale from the Mahabharata eerily mirrors boardrooms, parliaments, and homes today—where choices are made not with virtue, but with veiled agendas.

In corporate boardrooms, decisions that affect thousands are often made in the name of "efficiency," while the true motive may be profit at any cost. Layoffs are framed as restructuring, monopolies as mergers, and betrayals as bold leadership. The dice are rolled in closed-door meetings, far from those who'll pay the price.

In parliaments, alliances shift overnight, not out of ideology, but out of ambition. Political deals are sealed not in the interest of the people, but in the interest of power. Promises are made for votes, and then quietly discarded. Shakuni's cunning is alive—in every backroom negotiation.

Even within homes, tradition is sometimes used to silence dissent or justify injustice. Like Draupadi, many are offered up—women denied agency, youth forced into careers they didn't choose, or elders pushed aside in decisions about their own lives. Silence is mistaken for consent, and duty is demanded without fairness.

Whether it's corporate betrayal masked as strategy, or silent complicity dressed as tradition, the dice are still rolling—often loaded, often unjust. And like Yudhishthir, many today keep playing long after the cost has turned human.

When morality becomes negotiable and silence is mistaken for strength, even a game can destroy lives. In the grand court of Hastinapur, it wasn't just the dice that were crooked—the hearts behind them were too

CHAPTER 14

DISROBING TO CHASTISE

The Veiled Nature of Morality

In the Mahabharata, the episode of Draupadi's disrobing serves as a profound commentary on the complexities of morality, honor, and societal values. It highlights how actions perceived as private or personal can be manipulated for public humiliation, shedding light on the intricate dynamics of respect, power, and integrity. This incident underscores the vulnerability of individuals to the whims of those in power and the consequences of moral decay within a society.

The Game of Dice and Its Consequences

Draupadi, the noble wife of the Pandavas, had already endured the loss of her husband's kingdom due to the game of dice. When Yudhishthir, out of his inability to break the chains of his own optimism and pride, staked and lost his kingdom, the consequences quickly spiraled into something far worse. What was once a political game transformed into an immoral act of physical and emotional abuse.

In the court of Hastinapur, as Draupadi was dragged by her hair, her dignity was stripped away by the very men who were supposed to protect her. Duryodhan, instigated by Karna and his maternal uncle Shakuni, ordered the humiliating act of disrobing her, as a form of revenge for her rejection of Duryodhan in the

Swayamvar. Despite her pleas for mercy, no one, not even the respected elders like Bhishma, Dronacharya, or Kripacharya, came to her defense. They stood silent, watching as she was subjected to this degrading act.

Divine Intervention and Human Inaction

In the midst of her suffering, Draupadi turned to the divine for help. Her heartful cries reached Krishna, who intervened and miraculously extended the length of her saree, preventing her from being disrobed. The efforts of Duryodhan and his allies proved futile, as the cloth seemed endless, thwarting their attempts and ultimately exhausting them. Krishna's divine intervention restored Draupadi's dignity, reminding the court of Hastinapur that justice often comes from forces beyond human control.Draupadi's ordeal exposes the moral bankruptcy of the Kauravas and catalyzes the ensuing conflict. It also highlights the vulnerability and resilience of women in a patriarchal society. Her steadfast devotion to Krishna showcases the transformative power of unwavering faith in the face of adversity.

From Hastinapur to Modern Conflict Zones: The Battlefield of a Woman's Body

The disrobing of Draupadi is not confined to the grand sabha of Hastinapur. Her humiliation continues—in war-torn villages, in refugee camps, in conflict zones across the world, where women's bodies become battlegrounds for power, revenge, and dominance. Sexual violence against women during wars is not collateral damage—it is calculated cruelty. Rape, forced pregnancies, sexual enslavement, and torture are wielded like weapons by male perpetrators—soldiers, officers, and even civilians—who are emboldened by silence, impunity, and patriarchal systems that see women not as individuals, but as symbols of communities to be broken.

Much like Draupadi, countless women today stand alone in their cries for justice, surrounded by bystanders in positions of power. Promises of international protection and gender equality exist on paper, but the political will to implement them often fades in the face of entrenched misogyny. The silence of the Kaurava court is mirrored by global institutions that fail to act decisively—even as women and girls are violated in wars they did not start, and punished for identities they did not choose.

The disrobing of Draupadi is both a literal and symbolic act—stripping not just garments, but dignity, agency, and voice. And though Krishna came to her aid, the world cannot wait for divine intervention. Justice must be human-led and human-delivered.

As long as a woman's body remains the cheapest battlefield, every war—ancient or modern—is a war against humanity itself. And every silence in the face of that violence echoes the sabha of Hastinapur, where one woman stood alone, asking a question the world still struggles to answer.

CHAPTER 15

BHISHM PITAMAH: THE PARADOX OF PRINCIPLES

The Silent Practitioner of Gita's Philosophy

Long before Lord Krishna advised Arjun on the battlefield of Kurukshetra to perform one's duty without attachment to the fruits of action, Devavrat, later known as Bhishma Pitamah, had already been living this philosophy. A scion of the Kuru dynasty and the son of Ganga and King Shantanu, Bhishma stood as a symbol of duty, sacrifice, and unwavering resolve. His devotion to righteousness and dharma was admired across kingdoms—but beneath this veneer of idealism lay troubling contradictions.

The Vow That Shaped a Kingdom

Bhishma's early life was marked by a monumental sacrifice. To fulfill his father's desire to marry Satyavati, whose father insisted that only her sons should inherit the throne, Devavrat took a terrible vow of lifelong celibacy and renounced his claim to the crown. This singular act earned him the title "Bhishma," meaning "he of the strong vow." It was a selfless act in appearance—an extraordinary renunciation—but one that set in motion a lineage crisis that plagued the Kuru dynasty.

The Blind Eye to Injustice

Bhishma's personal sense of duty, however, often blinded him to the broader moral failures unfolding around him. He upheld his vow, but in doing so, failed to act when his intervention could have averted tragedy. When his half-brother died childless, Satyavati pleaded with Bhishma to marry the widowed queen and protect the dynasty. Yet again, he declined—honoring his personal vow over the desperate needs of his family and kingdom.

Warrior Without Moral Intervention

He later abducted the princesses of Kashi to secure a marriage alliance for his half-brother—an act that brought him into conflict with his own guru, Parshurama. His righteousness, though severe, lacked empathy. Amba, one of the princesses, was caught in this web of patriarchy, leading her to a path of vengeance and eventual rebirth as Shikhandi. Bhishma's hands, while raised in blessing, were equally complicit in others' suffering.

The Disrobing of Draupadi: A Deafening Silence

The moment that shattered all illusions of Bhishma's nobility was his silence during Draupadi's disrobing. As the grand patriarch and commander-in-chief, his voice held weight—but he chose to remain a mute spectator as a woman was dragged and humiliated in court. He was not blind like Dhritarashtra; his eyes witnessed the vulgarity of Duryodhana slapping his thigh and inviting Draupadi to sit upon it. Yet

Bhishma—protector of dharma—stood still. A man capable of waging war against his guru failed to raise his voice against injustice to a woman.

This was no passive failing; it was an active betrayal of the very values he claimed to uphold.

The Final Reckoning

During the Kurukshetra war, Bhishma led the Kaurava army with unmatched skill, nearly decimating the Pandava forces. Krishna, though bound by his vow not to lift arms, contemplated breaking it just to stop him. Eventually, Arjun, guided by Shikhandi, brought Bhishma down—not through dishonor, but through strategy. Bhishma, lying on a bed of arrows, chose to delay death until an auspicious moment, wielding the boon of *iccha-mrityu*.

As he lay wounded, reflecting on life, his mind carried the weight of what he had not done as much as what he had done.

The Modern Sabha: Bhishmas Among Us

In the court of Hastinapur, Bhishma sat still—a man of power, wisdom, and immense influence—watching Draupadi's humiliation unfold. He chose his vow over his voice, dharma over justice, silence over resistance. And in doing so, he allowed evil to triumph while virtue was stripped bare.

Today, we don't need to look far to see modern-day Bhishmas—those who wield enormous influence, who command platforms that reach millions, and yet remain mute in the face of blatant injustice. Whether it is the silencing of dissent, the targeting of vulnerable communities, or the erosion of basic human rights—our celebrities, athletes, industrialists, and icons often watch from the galleries of privilege, cloaked in the silence of convenience.

When citizens rise to demand dignity and justice, when institutions begin to crack, when moral lines are blurred—these powerful voices often recede. Their silence isn't neutral; it is a signal. A choice to side with comfort over conscience, brand over bravery.

In many parts of the world, we see prominent figures taking a stand—using stages, screens, and stadiums to speak truth to power. Their solidarity can amplify the unheard, their words can sway public sentiment, and their courage can ignite movements. But where this spirit is absent, the silence of the influential becomes not just disappointing, but dangerous.

Like Bhishma, many justify their quietude with claims of neutrality, professional responsibility, or fear of backlash. But silence in the face of injustice is not neutrality—it is complicity.The absence of such vocal solidarity from those in power is deafening. They continue to rake in profits, adoration, and clout—gifts given by the very society now gasping for justice—while refusing to risk even a word. And like Bhishma, they justify their silence as duty to their careers, investors, or apolitical identities. But silence in the face of moral crisis is not neutrality. It is endorsement.

Bhishma's silence did not protect Hastinapur. It condemned it.

The silence of today's icons will not protect society. It will corrode its conscience.

In honoring his vows, Bhishma Pitamah upheld his image, but not always his integrity—for true nobility lies not in silence or sacrifice alone, but in the courage to speak and act when justice is under assault.

CHAPTER 16

THE PANDAVAS' EXILE – A JOURNEY OF RESILIENCE AND RIGHTEOUSNESS

The Ordeal of Exile: A Test Beyond the Battlefield

Exile, a profound form of displacement, strips individuals of their identity, status, and homeland. In the Mahabharata, the Pandavas' exile was not merely a physical journey but a crucible that tested their virtues, resilience, and adherence to dharma. Banished due to a deceitful game of dice orchestrated by Duryodhana, they embarked on a 13-year odyssey—12 years in the forest followed by a year incognito. The Pandavas' exile was not a consequence of military defeat but stemmed from a manipulated game of dice orchestrated by Shakuni and Duryodhana. Despite the evident treachery, King Dhritarashtra remained passive, failing to uphold justice. It was a significant lapse in moral leadership, where personal biases overshadowed the principles of dharma This period was not just about survival but about preserving honor, unity, and purpose amidst adversity. The Pandavas' exile is not just a tale of hardship but a testament to the human spirit's capacity to endure, adapt, and uphold righteousness.

Embracing Anonymity: The Incognito Year in Matsya

The thirteenth year, known as *Agyatvasa*, required the Pandavas to live undetected in the kingdom of Matsya.

Assuming humble roles—Yudhishthira as a courtier of king Virat, Bhima as a cook, Arjuna as a dance teacher, Nakula and Sahadeva as caretakers of horses and cattle, and Draupadi as a maid—they concealed their royal identities. This phase was a profound exercise in humility and adaptability, challenging them to uphold their principles without the privileges of their past.

Trials in Disguise: Confronting Injustice

Even in anonymity, the Pandavas faced moral dilemmas. Draupadi's harassment by Kichaka, the powerful commander of Matsya, tested their commitment to justice. Bhima's killing of Kichaka was a bold act to protect Draupadi's dignity without compromising their incognito status. Such incidents underscore the constant tension between upholding dharma and ensuring survival.

Revelation and Alliance: The Path to Reclamation

Upon completing their incognito year, the Pandavas revealed their identities to King Virata. This disclosure not only marked the end of their exile but also forged a crucial alliance for the impending Kurukshetra war. The marriage of Arjun's son, Abhimanyu, to Virata's daughter, Uttara, further solidified this bond, setting the stage for their return to power.

Exile Rewritten: The Modern-Day Displacement of the Pandavas

The Pandavas once ruled a kingdom. With strength, wisdom, and dharma by their side, they were symbols of righteous leadership. But a single game—one unfair, fateful throw of dice—left them homeless. Banished. Forced to wander forests, stripped of titles, security, and dignity.

That ancient exile is not so ancient anymore.

Today, millions walk similar paths—not as princes but as displaced people. Like the Pandavas, they are not just victims of chance, but of systems rigged against them: wars not of their making, storms not of their summoning, borders that close while bombs fall, or projects that rise while homes fall. Their kingdoms lost are their homes—swept away by conflict, swallowed by flood, or emptied by fear.

They carry no crown, only the weight of memory.

In 2024, nearly 65% of acutely food-insecure people lived in fragile or conflict-affected regions, many of them forcibly displaced. Their exile is compounded by hunger, statelessness, and a crisis of identity. Just as the Pandavas faced wild beasts, harsh forests, and uncertain allies, the displaced of today must navigate refugee camps, unfamiliar cultures, and invisible barriers of discrimination.

The forest of exile today is not green—it is grey, overcrowded, fenced. It smells of tarpaulin and fatigue.

Across the globe, stories echo this theme:

- **Kashmiri Pandits**, once deeply rooted in the cultural and spiritual landscape of the Kashmir Valley, were forced to flee in the early 1990s due to a wave of militancy and targeted violence. Decades later, many still live in exile—within their own country—yearning for home and justice.

- **Syrian refugees**, fleeing a brutal civil war, have scattered across the Middle East and Europe. Generations born in exile now grow up in limbo—neither fully home nor fully accepted where they are.
- **The Rohingya people**, driven from Myanmar by persecution and violence, have sought refuge in crowded camps in Bangladesh, stateless and vulnerable.
- **Ukrainians**, displaced by the ongoing conflict, have become refugees in their own land and across Europe, carrying trauma, loss, and uncertainty along with their national pride.
- **South Sudanese families**, caught in waves of civil war and climate disasters, have endured repeated cycles of displacement, famine, and rebuilding.

And like the Pandavas, today's exiled people hold on to stories. Stories of lands left behind. Languages fading on the tongues of their children. Rituals re-enacted in cramped corners. Memories turned into maps of return.

But exile is not just about leaving—it's about being forgotten. And just as the Pandavas were betrayed by silence and complicity, the displaced today are often unseen in policy papers and ignored in prime-time debates. Their exile becomes not just physical, but existential.

Yet, the most powerful thread connecting the ancient and the modern is resilience.

The Pandavas did not crumble in the forest. They trained, they reflected, they grew. Today's displaced—whether in conflict zones, climate-hit regions, or within the borders of their own country—show the same grit. They rebuild, teach their children under tents, cook with borrowed spices, vote with hope, and dream of return.

They may have no kingdom, but they have not lost their spirit.

Exile is not only about what is lost—it is about what is carried forward.

The displaced of today, like the Pandavas of yesterday, carry the blueprints of a return – not just to land, but to dignity.

CHAPTER 17

THE EXILE'S END: DIPLOMACY DESTROYED BY EGO

A Hope for Peace

After their years in exile, the Pandavas allied with King Virat following Uttara's marriage to Abhimanyu. Hoping to avoid war, Yudhishthir sought a peaceful settlement with King Dhritarashtra to reclaim Indraprastha. He decided to send a diplomatic envoy instead of going himself and travelled to Dwarika to seek Krishna's guidance.

Krishna, wise in the ways of human behavior and politics, advised against Yudhishthir's personal visit. Instead, he suggested sending a carefully chosen messenger—one endowed with clarity, courtesy, and conviction—similar to how Rama had once sent Angad to negotiate with Ravan.

The Messenger's Reception

The envoy, well-briefed and respectful, reached Hastinapur and requested an audience with Dhritarashtra. However, the king was upset because Yudhishthir hadn't come in person and viewed it as arrogance. The messenger was told to wait and appear in court the next day, as per protocol.

In court, filled with advisors and ministers, the envoy respectfully conveyed Yudhishthir's message: the

Pandavas had completed their exile and now humbly sought the return of their rightful kingdom. Dhritarashtra dismissed the plea, calling it an undignified demand lacking humility, and sent the messenger away empty-handed.

A Realization and Another Attempt

When the messenger returned and reported the court proceedings, Yudhishthir deeply regretted not meeting Dhritarashtra himself. He recognized his failure to uphold the behavior expected when addressing an elder, especially a father's brother. He wished to go personally and apologize. But Krishna, sensing the futility, stepped in to take on the negotiation himself.

Krishna was aware of the values Kunti had instilled in her sons—restraint, virtue, and respectful conduct. But he also knew that Dhritarashtra's decision would be final, leaving no room for second chances.

Krishna at Hastinapur

Krishna journeyed to Hastinapur, accompanied by Satyaki of the Narayan Sena. Though warmly received, Krishna rejected the royal comforts arranged by Duryodhan and instead stayed at Vidura's humble home. Vidura's wife, in ecstatic devotion, mistakenly offered Krishna banana peels instead of fruit—but Krishna accepted them with joy. Her devotion mattered more than her offering. A timeless truth: sincere intentions outweigh grand gestures.

Before entering the court, Vidura shared that he had earlier advised Dhritarashtra to crown Yudhishthir to end the conflict—but his proposal was swiftly dismissed by Dronacharya and the others.

The Final Plea

In court, Krishna addressed the king and his advisors with composed dignity:

"The Pandavas, in the prime of their youth, renounced pleasure and endured exile with grace. They adhered to every term, even when tempted to rebel. Such discipline is rare. In light of their sacrifice, I urge you to return Indraprastha and, if possible, grant them four nearby villages—Panprastha, Vyaghrapatha, Tilprastha, and Swarnprastha—for their sustenance." So they asked for 5 villages - Indraprastha (Delhi), Tilprastha (Tilpat), Swarnprastha (Sonipat), Panprastha (Panipat), and Vyaghrprastha (Baghpat).

Dhritarashtra listened but passed the responsibility to Duryodhan.

Duryodhan, unmoved, replied:

"They broke the terms of exile by revealing themselves prematurely. They must return to the forest. I will not yield the crown."

Krishna tried once more:

"Even if they disclosed their identity a day early, it wasn't public. It could be an error in calculation. We must not punish ignorance with injustice."

Duryodhan remained adamant. Krishna then gave his final word:

"My counsel was for the good of all. But your blindness to reason and your fear-driven actions will lead to ruin. If mutual loyalty and fairness cannot prevail, war will be the only recourse. Prepare yourself."

Modern-Day Kurukshetra: When Diplomacy Fails and War Begin

In the *Mahabharata,* Lord Krishna—divine statesman, philosopher, and the ultimate diplomat—undertook one final mission of peace. As a neutral emissary, he offered reconciliation, compromise, and the wisdom of dharma to avoid war. His proposals were dismissed, mocked, and ultimately rejected by Duryodhana, who even attempted to imprison him. With dialogue collapsing, the only path left was that of war—the cataclysmic Kurukshetra.

Over two millennia later, modern diplomacy echoes Krishna's journey. States send envoys, negotiate accords, host summits, and invoke global institutions. Yet, when egos tower over empathy and national interest overshadows shared humanity, diplomacy collapses. War, once again, becomes the language of failed understanding.

21st-Century Diplomacy: Between Idealism and Realism

As L.G. Dilini Tharika Siriwardana outlines, modern diplomacy treads an increasingly complex terrain. Shaped by globalization, technological disruption, and a shifting world order, diplomacy today must juggle idealistic intentions with realist strategies. Yet despite this evolution, the core principle remains unchanged: diplomacy is an alternative to war.

But what happens when this alternative fails?

Tony Benn's assertion—*"War is the ultimate failure of diplomacy"*—becomes the chilling verdict of international crises. The fall of diplomacy in Iraq, the breakdown in Syria, and the persistent stalemate in the Israel-Palestine conflict—each stands as a contemporary Kurukshetra where modern Krishnas were ignored, ridiculed, or outmaneuvered.

When States Choose Duryodhana Over Dharma

Consider the Iraq War. Diplomacy was not given a genuine chance. Unverified claims, unilateral actions, and ideological overreach led to military intervention with long-term global repercussions. Similarly, in Syria, international diplomacy drowned in conflicting interests, vetoes, and half-hearted interventions, leading to a humanitarian catastrophe.

North Korea and Iran, too, reveal how diplomacy—when reduced to threats and sanctions without mutual respect—fails to de-escalate conflict. The United States' abandonment of multilateral agreements, like the Iran nuclear deal, has often mirrored Duryodhana's obstinance: rejecting middle paths in favor of power plays.

In Ukraine, as in the Balkans decades before, diplomacy was unable to preempt war. Even as envoys met and treaties were signed, the undercurrent of strategic mistrust and territorial ambition led to armed conflict. Once again, the battlefield trumped the negotiating table.

Failures Not Just of Process, But of People

Siriwardana insightfully notes that diplomacy often fails due to "*the personal failure of leading players responsible for foreign policy.*" Historical anecdotes, like the bias of French Foreign Minister Delcassé or Russian envoy Hartwig's provocations, mirror today's impasses where personal ideologies, nationalism, and political gains override rational compromise.

As in the Mahabharat where Krishna's wisdom was cast aside due to pride, today's leaders sometimes ignore their diplomats, disregard civil society voices, or dismiss non-state voices. The result? A breakdown in trust, a hardening of positions, and the slow march toward violence.

Lessons from Kurukshetra: Reclaiming Diplomacy's Moral Compass

The Mahabharat offers a timeless warning: when dialogue is dismissed as weakness and compromise is seen as defeat, war becomes inevitable. But it also offers a blueprint. Krishna's attempt at peace, though rejected, was not in vain—it set the moral groundwork that legitimized the war and clarified the stakes.

Modern diplomacy must embrace this duality. It must be both idealistic and strategic—firm in values, flexible in approach. Leaders must value diplomacy not as mere protocol but as a sacred tool of statecraft. As Sun Tzu said, "*The supreme art of war is to subdue the enemy without fighting."* But subduing an enemy requires empathy, understanding, and patience—traits often lost in political calculations.

We must learn from past failures. As Krishna stood between war and peace, offering dharma as the path forward, so must today's diplomats and leaders stand resolute—not only against war, but for the dignity of dialogue.

Because when the modern-day Krishna —a wise and peace-seeking leader— walks into a global forum with outstretched hands, and the world turns its back—Kurukshetra may not be far behind.

Ignore the hand of dialogue, and you may awaken the fist of destiny.

CHAPTER 18

THE STATURE OF STANCE: WHEN DEMEANOR DEFINES DESTINY

Support Seeking Mission

As the clouds of war darkened over Kurukshetra, both the Kauravas and Pandavas began rallying support from neighboring kingdoms. Though the date of battle was not yet set, the urgency was palpable.

Understanding Krishna's divine influence and political sway, Duryodhana hurried to seek his favor. He reached Krishna's abode and found him asleep. Eager to appear first, Duryodhana positioned himself by Krishna's head and waited patiently for him to wake.

Not long after, Yudhishthira arrived with the same intent but humbly stood near Krishna's feet. Upon waking, Krishna saw Yudhishthira first and then noticed Duryodhana. After greeting both, he inquired about the purpose of their visit.

Both had come with the same aim: to request Krishna's support in the impending war.

Krishna responded with calm dignity, "I cannot side with both. On one side, I will be present in person, but I shall not lift any weapon. On the other, my Narayani Sena—my powerful army—will be given. Since I saw Yudhishthira first, I shall offer him the first choice."

Demonstrating his characteristic humility, Yudhishthira said, "Since Duryodhana came before me, he should choose first."

But Krishna remained firm: behavior, not order of arrival, mattered. By choosing to stand at the feet instead of the head, Yudhishthira had revealed not just his presence, but reverence too. He had come to seek, not to demand.

Eventually, Yudhishthira chose Krishna himself, despite the fact that he would not fight. Duryodhana, pleased by what he believed was a shrewd choice, chose the vast Narayani Sena.

The Humility in One's Stance

This episode imparts a profound lesson: our physical stance often mirrors our inner disposition. In the Ramayana, after defeating Ravan, Rama instructed Lakshman to seek wisdom from the dying demon king. Lakshman approached and stood near Ravana's head, but Ravan, perceiving this as arrogance, refused to speak. When Rama approached and humbly sat near Ravana's feet, Ravan, moved by this gesture, shared his knowledge.

This narrative underscores that true wisdom is often granted to those who approach with humility and respect.

Modern Reflections: When Ego Leads, Wisdom Bleeds

In the Mahabharata, Yudhishthir stood humbly near Krishna's feet—not out of weakness, but out of wisdom. He knew that titles meant little before truth. He sought guidance, not validation.

True leaders, like Krishna, look beyond appearances. They assess intent, humility, and conduct—qualities sorely missing in many modern negotiations. Whether it's a nation seeking peace or an employee seeking mentorship, the approach often reveals more than the request itself.

Ego continues to sit by the head, while wisdom quietly waits at the feet.

In today's world, the modern Yudhishthir might be a CEO who enters a high-stakes negotiation not with arrogance, but with open ears—acknowledging what he doesn't know, inviting feedback, and sitting beside his juniors to understand the ground reality.

He doesn't mistake his position for perfection. Like Yudhishthir, he knows that humility isn't thinking less of himself, but thinking of himself less. He listens more than he speaks. He reflects when criticised, shows up on time, looks people in the eye, and never forgets—ego blinds, but humility reveals.

The wisest in the room is rarely the loudest—he's the one who knows when to kneel and when to lead.

CHAPTER 19

THE BLIND SPOT OF POWER: WHEN VISION LACKS VALUES

The Gift Of Remote Vision

In the royal court of Hastinapur, Sanjay stood as a trusted and insightful minister—disciple of Sage Ved Vyas and blessed with ***Divya Drishti***, a divine gift that allowed him to witness distant events as if he were physically present. When the great war of Kurukshetra erupted, Sanjay remained by the side of the blind King Dhritarashtra, describing every detail of the battlefield—each clash of swords, strategic move, and emotional turn—as though he were transmitting a live telecast. Long before the advent of modern technology, it was Sanjay's yogic power and focused awareness that brought the battlefield into the palace, bridging miles through the strength of mind and spirit.

Blindness Beyond Sight

The divine gift granted to Sanjaya was a marvel—but its use revealed a deeper tragedy. King Dhritarashtra, blind by birth and blinded further by attachment, was given this extraordinary chance to witness the battlefield—not with the curiosity of a just ruler, but with the anxiety of a possessive father. He never once asked about the pain of the mothers—Gandhari or Kunti—or showed concern for the thousands of soldiers fighting and dying under his command.

Though he was granted the rare opportunity to witness truth in real time through Sanjay's vision, he failed to see what truly mattered: compassion, justice, and moral responsibility. His was a gaze that saw everything, yet understood nothing.

Sight Without Soul: From Dhritarashtra to the Digital Age

In the Mahabharata, Sanjay narrated the war of Kurukshetra in vivid, heart-wrenching detail to a blind Dhritarashtra, who, despite knowing the carnage and loss unfolding, remained unmoved—his only concern: the fate of his own children. This ancient tale finds unsettling resonance in our modern age, where technology offers us an omniscient lens into global crises—wars livestreamed, violations documented in real time, suffering captured in pixels. Yet like Dhritarashtra, power often watches passively, trapped in self-interest.

Today, we don't need divine sight; we have drones, satellites, generative AI, and deepfakes. The battlefield is no longer Kurukshetra—it is Gaza, Ukraine, or a virtual server flooded with non-consensual images, many weaponized against women. Yet the outcome is eerily similar: information without intervention, awareness without accountability.

On the 25th anniversary of the Universal Declaration of Human Rights, the Society for Computers and Law was born—symbolizing hope that the digital revolution would be guided by human dignity. Yet in the decades since, human rights have too often played second fiddle to ethical debates and corporate interest. The rise of AI, data surveillance, and image-based abuse has exposed the deep tension between what we *can* do and what we *should* protect.

Generative AI systems now replicate historical biases, amplify discrimination, and create harmful content. Deepfakes—over 90% of which target women in sexually exploitative ways—blur the line between entertainment and violation. Article 8 of the European Convention on Human Rights, which safeguards privacy and data dignity, is routinely tested by technologies that can manipulate identities and realities. Still, regulatory frameworks lag behind, and justice remains reactive.

Governments, like Dhritarashtra, often listen to detailed briefings of human suffering—whether from war zones or digital platforms—yet act only when political capital is at stake. Just as Dhritarashtra wept for his sons but not for the thousands dying under their command, today's institutions react with concern when their interests are threatened, but remain indifferent to the broader human toll. The pain of "others" is often noted, never felt.

In war, leaders once feared public backlash spurred by graphic imagery—the so-called "body-bag effect." Now, sanitized, remote, and digitally filtered warcraft allows a disengaged populace to accept violence as abstraction. The horror, once a deterrent, is now deleted with a click. Atrocities are now hidden behind algorithms, keeping public conscience comfortably disengaged.

This disengagement, while convenient, is dangerous. It breeds apathy. It normalizes harm. It allows war, abuse, and discrimination to persist under a veneer of control.

The lesson from Sanjay and Dhritarashtra is enduring: seeing without feeling is a betrayal of humanity. Vision must not stop at observation—it must lead to compassion, to responsibility, to reform. Otherwise, we risk becoming a society with eyes wide open, and hearts tightly shut.

This is the age of Sanjay 2.0—hyperconnected, hyper-aware—but with a world full of Dhritarashtras, blind not in vision, but in values.

The lesson is clear: technological power must be coupled with moral clarity. Seeing is not enough. Feeling is essential. Action, even more so. For if we continue to look without conscience, we risk becoming spectators in a world collapsing beneath the weight of our own indifference.

When vision serves ego and not empathy, it becomes a weapon—not a window. The Mahabharata teaches us that true leadership lies not in how much we see, but in how deeply we feel for what we see.

Technology may sharpen our vision, but only values can give it direction.

CHAPTER 20

FROM CONCH SHELLS TO MISSILES: THE SHIFTING ETHICS OF WAR

Awaiting the First Blow: Then and Now

As the armies of the Kauravas and Pandavas assembled at Kurukshetra, conches were blown, marking the beginning of a historic war. The ancient battlefield was a stage for valor, vengeance, and dharma—or at least the appearance of it. Unlike modern wars, these battles were often fought in open spaces, removed from civilian settlements. The warriors knew their opponents, and the war ended when one side surrendered or was defeated. The conflict, while violent, still bore traces of personal honor, duty, and accountability.

Origins of Conflict: A Primitive Impulse

The earliest form of war emerged as a means of survival. In ancient times, humans fought mainly to protect themselves—from wild animals or from others who threatened their food and shelter. As small groups of people settled and began forming communities, they needed land to grow crops and water to survive. Naturally, disputes arose when neighboring groups competed for the same fertile lands or hunting areas.

These early conflicts were not based on any formal military strategy. They were raw, instinctive reactions to immediate threats. But as populations grew and communities expanded, so did their desire for control, status, and resources. Defending territory became more than just a need—it became a matter of pride and power. Eventually, these basic survival clashes evolved into organized wars, as seen in grand epics like the Mahabharata.

Kurukshetra: A War Where Ethics Clashed with Ego

The battle of Kurukshetra was not merely a political conflict—it was a war fueled by the unyielding arrogance of the Kauravas. Despite the Pandavas' rightful claim to their kingdom, their appeals were denied. What should have been resolved through dialogue escalated into war because noble conduct and statesmanship were absent. The war became inevitable, not due to lack of alternatives, but due to lack of behavioral intent—the willingness to compromise, empathize, or act with fairness.

Humanitarian Spirit in Ancient Battles

Even in ancient times, wars sometimes carried a sense of moral duty. Warriors often fought on behalf of the weak, the voiceless, and those who had no means to protect their land or dignity. They fought not only for territory but for identity—shared cultures, values, and ways of life. Though brutal, ancient warfare retained a thread of human connection and clarity in its cause.

Modern Warfare: Sophistication Without Soul

Today, warfare has transformed into a highly advanced and complex system driven by science, politics, and profit. It is no longer limited to traditional battlefields far from everyday life. Instead, war now reaches right into cities, homes, and even cyberspace. Airstrikes, drone attacks, cyberattacks, and long-range missiles have replaced face-to-face combat, making destruction faster and more impersonal.

Arjuna's moral paralysis before the war wasn't cowardice—it was conscience. Modern warfare lacks that moment of stillness. We no longer ask, "Should I fight?" We ask, "How fast can I win?"

No side fully wears the white of virtue or the black of evil. Just as Duryodhana believed his cause was just, modern leaders invoke national security, religion, or historical grievance to justify warfare.

Unlike in ancient times, where battles were often fought away from civilian areas and involved only warriors, modern wars cause widespread harm to ordinary people. Entire populations are displaced, civilian homes and hospitals are bombed, and the destruction of essential infrastructure—like power grids and water supplies—is dismissed as "collateral damage."

While technology gives us instant access to intelligence and real-time updates, it hasn't made us wiser in preventing war. In many cases, this advanced machinery is used not to protect, but to assert dominance, exploit resources, or display power—often with little regard for human suffering.

The Modern Dilemma: Technological Might Without Moral Muscle

We live in an era where nations possess weapons capable of ending civilizations, yet often lack the ethical compass to use their power responsibly. Alliances, nationalism, and imperial ambitions continue to drive conflicts. Disputes over borders, minerals, and water sources escalate into full-scale wars. In some cases, allied countries thousands of miles away become targets, dragging innocents into chaos.

With satellite-guided missiles, surveillance drones, and media propaganda, modern war is waged not just on land, but in the air, sea, and cyberspace. And often, it's not just nations fighting—but ideologies, egos, and economic interests.

Lessons from the Past: What the Mahabharata Still Teaches Us

The Mahabharata reminds us that war is rarely just about weapons—it is about choices. And when leaders abandon noble conduct and behavioral ethics, destruction is inevitable—no matter how advanced the tools they wield. Kurukshetra was born not out of lack of options but out of refusal to act with humility and justice.

The Mahabharata ended not in victory but in **mourning**. The Pandavas won their kingdom, but lost their sons, allies, and joy. The battlefield became a graveyard of regret.

Modern wars might end in treaties, but the scars remain:

- Afghanistan was 'won' and then abandoned.
- Syria remains a chessboard of foreign interests.
- Palestine burns in cycles.

We, like the characters of the Mahabharata, are caught in the illusion of victory—**but the soul knows otherwise**.

A New Code of Dharma?

The Mahabharata was not just a tale of war—it was a mirror. It warned us of the cost of pride, revenge, and moral compromise. Today, the mirror is in our hands—flashing on newsfeeds, filled with suffering civilians and euphemisms like "surgical strike" and "collateral damage."

The epic dared to question the very act of war even while enacting it. Can we, in our age of satellites and cyber war, ask those questions again?

Can we write a new war code?

Not based on self-righteous narratives or ancient hatreds, but on:

- Restraint over revenge
- Empathy over enmity
- Wisdom over weaponry

Until we do, every missile launched is just another arrow shot on the plains of Kurukshetra.

And we are all Arjunas—hesitant, haunted, and still looking for Krishna.

Technology may have reshaped the battlefield, but it cannot substitute for character. Until leaders across ages learn that wars are won not by might alone but by moral clarity, humanity will continue to repeat the same blood-stained mistakes—only with sharper blades and longer shadows.

CHAPTER 21

THE BATTLEFIELD OF KURUKSHETRA: A WAR OF SELF-INTEREST

The Stage for Conflict

On the eve of the great war in Kurukshetra, the Pandavas and Kauravas stood face to face, preparing for battle. Arjun, seated on his chariot with the fluttering flag bearing the image of Lord Hanuman, was ready to lead his troops. The sight of Lord Hanuman on the flag symbolized divine presence, reminding all that no battle, especially one as significant as this, was fought without the presence of higher powers. Lord Krishna served as Arjun's charioteer. At Arjun's request, Krishna drove the chariot into the heart of the battlefield, positioning it between the two opposing armies.

A Moment of Reflection

From the center of the battlefield, Arjun surveyed the forces arrayed against him. There, in the enemy ranks, he saw familiar faces—Bhishma Pitamah, Dronacharya, and other respected elders and warriors who had allied with Duryodhana. Arjun's heart filled with compassion as he recognized that those he would have to fight were his family—his elders, teachers, and cousins. Overcome with grief and confusion, he turned to Krishna and expressed his deep inner turmoil.

Arjun questioned the very nature of the war. What good was victory if it meant the destruction of his family? What was the value of a kingdom that came at the cost of such suffering and death? He felt conflicted, torn between his duty as a warrior and his love for his kith and kin. The idea of killing those he cherished for the sake of a kingdom seemed unthinkable. In his despair, Arjun laid down his bow and arrow, declaring that he could not fight. He chose, in that moment, to abandon the battlefield, unwilling to participate in a war that would annihilate his family and destroy his heritage.

A King's Blindness to Greater Truths

King Dhritarashtra was blind by birth—but his lack of vision went far beyond the physical. Seated in the palace of Hastinapur, he could not see the battlefield with his eyes, but even more tragically, he failed to see with wisdom, compassion, or foresight.

His physical blindness was not his fault—but his emotional blindness, his refusal to rise above personal attachments, was a failure of character. Unlike Arjun, who paused to question the morality of killing his own kin, Dhritarashtra never once considered the broader cost of war.He ignored his role as a ruler, whose foremost duty was to uphold justice, peace, and dharma.

In the end, it wasn't his eyes that failed him. It was his heart, his judgment, and his understanding.

Modern Dhritarashtras: The Price of Self-Interest

In the *Mahabharat,* King Dhritarashtra stands as a stark symbol of destructive self-interest—his love for his sons clouded his judgment, making him blind not only in vision but in conscience. Today, his legacy endures—not in palaces and war councils, but in presidential suites, corporate boardrooms, and policy chambers.

Self-Interest: The Modern Driving Force

In the modern world, self-interest—be it personal, political, or national—continues to shape key decisions. Leaders prioritize electoral victories, image management, or short-term economic growth over long-term welfare. Countries compete not for collective upliftment but for strategic advantage, often treating international partnerships as zero-sum games. A **2024 Munich Security Conference survey** revealed that nations today define success not by the global good but in comparison to each other, measuring victory in relative gains rather than shared progress.

This worldview mirrors Dhritarashtra's obsession with ensuring his son Duryodhana's dominance, even if it meant the destruction of an entire kingdom.

The Ethical Collapse

When political leaders, much like Dhritarashtra, focus narrowly on personal or party loyalty, governance suffers. During crises like the **COVID-19 pandemic**, some nations hoarded medical supplies, underplayed risks, or distorted data to protect their leadership's image—actions that cost lives and deepened mistrust. This myopic self-preservation echoes the blind king's refusal to intervene, even as his silence led to war.

In business, scandals like Enron or the 2008 global financial crisis revealed how corporate elites placed profits over people, pushing millions into unemployment and poverty. These were not mere financial miscalculations but ethical failures—decisions rooted in greed and a disregard for consequence.

Geopolitics and the Cost of Dominance

Wars are no longer about defense—they are often about resources, ideological projection, or geostrategic control. Conflicts in oil-rich regions or trade wars over technological dominance are examples of self-interest masquerading as national security. Innocent lives become collateral damage as global powers play out their versions of the *Kurukshetra.*

The Personal Sphere: Favoritism and Attachment

Even in families, the Dhritarashtra syndrome plays out. Favoritism, pride, and emotional attachments often guide decisions, leading to fractured relationships and generational rifts. Like the king who refused to see his nephews as his own blood, many parents and guardians fail to uphold fairness and emotional integrity.

A Contrast of Conscience: Arjun vs. Dhritarashtra

The *Mahabharat* offers another figure: Arjun. Standing at the brink of battle, he paused. He questioned. He wept. Unlike Dhritarashtra, he *saw*—not just with eyes, but with conscience. His moral dilemma reflects the responsibility that comes with power.

Our leaders, too, must ask: **Do we act like Dhritarashtra—fearing loss and blinded by attachment—or like Arjun—wrestling with conscience before taking action?**

The Tragedy of Our Time

The real tragedy of today is not conflict itself but the moral blindness that precedes it—the inability to look beyond the self. As Dhritarashtra clung to the illusion of protecting his family, he lost his kingdom. Nations today, in clinging to narrow self-interest, risk losing their humanity.

"The point is, ladies and gentlemen, that greed—for lack of a better word—is good," declared Gordon Gekko in *Wall Street* (1987), a pop culture ode to capitalism. But is it? History and scripture alike suggest otherwise: when self-interest eclipses ethical responsibility, civilizations crumble.

A Call for Enlightened Self-Interest

What if, instead, leaders embraced **enlightened self-interest**—where collaboration serves mutual benefit, and progress is measured not by dominance but by shared dignity?

It is time the world learned from Dhritarashtra—not by repeating his mistakes, but by recognizing their cost.

The enduring truth is this: real leadership demands the courage to rise above personal ties and choose principle over privilege.

Just as Arjun's fiercest battle was not with his enemies but within his conscience, so too is the greatest war of our times—fought not on battlefields, but in the silent spaces between self-interest and the greater good. Without noble intent, even the grandest of triumphs turns to dust.

CHAPTER 22

THE BATTLE WITHIN: THE TEST OF TRUE INTENT

Arjun's Inner Conflict

On the battlefield of Kurukshetra, Arjun stood paralyzed by anguish. With his bow slipping from his hand and his heart heavy, he faced a dilemma beyond the physical—a crisis of conscience. How could he raise his weapon against Bhishma and Dronacharya —men he had worshipped and loved?

In a voice filled with sorrow, Arjun said to Lord Krishna,

"I would rather live by begging than kill these noble elders. Even if I were to gain power, wealth, or the entire earth unchallenged, it would be stained with their blood. I am confused, unsure of what is right or wrong. I surrender to you—please guide me."

Krishna's Transcendental Revelation

Krishna, seeing Arjun's despair, responded not with pity, but with profound truth:

"You speak the words of wisdom, yet grieve for those who should not be grieved. The wise mourn neither the living nor the dead."

He reminded Arjun of the timeless nature of the soul—that it is eternal, imperishable, and untouched by weapons, fire, water, or wind. The body, Krishna said, is like a garment: worn out and discarded, only to be replaced. But the soul neither dies nor is born; it simply *is*.

The pain Arjun felt was rooted not in truth, but in illusion—a blindness to higher understanding, just as many others in the Mahabharata were blind to dharma in favor of personal attachments.

Krishna continued:

"Birth and death are inevitable. Wise men endure the joys and sorrows of life with equanimity, knowing that the soul is unchanged through it all. Your duty as a warrior is to fight for righteousness. To avoid this duty is not compassion—it is weakness."

The True Enemy: Blind Attachments

Krishna's words struck at the heart of the Mahabharat's central theme: most of the tragedy unfolded not from lack of power, but from lack of clarity, courage, and noble intent. Arjun was at least willing to question himself. In contrast, King Dhritarashtra, though physically blind, was even blinder in judgment—clinging to his sons despite their cruelty, refusing to uphold justice.

Arjun's struggle was not against the Kauravas alone—it was a battle within, between emotional attachments and righteous action. The moment he accepted Krishna's guidance, he stepped into his dharma, ready to fight not out of anger, but out of duty.

Modern Parallels: Leadership Without Vision

This eternal lesson remains painfully relevant today. In modern times, we see leaders—political, corporate, even within families—failing to act for the greater good due to personal ties or self-interest. Decisions are made not based on principle, but to protect power, wealth, or image.

For instance:

- A politician avoids taking action against corrupt colleagues to maintain party unity, risking public trust.
- A CEO turns a blind eye to unethical practices to protect quarterly profits, disregarding environmental damage or employee welfare.
- A parent favors one child blindly, even when that child causes harm, mirroring Dhritarashtra's mistake.

These are all modern-day Kurukshetras, where convenience triumphs over conscience, and society pays the price.

The Final Realization

Arjun's transformation wasn't about picking up his bow—it was about seeing with wisdom. He was no longer fighting for himself, but for a greater truth. The Mahabharata doesn't ask us to take sides in war; it asks us to reflect:

Are we choosing what's easy, or what's right?

True victory lies not in conquest, but in clarity of intent. Without noble purpose, even the most glorious triumphs are empty.

CHAPTER 23

THE COSMIC WARNING: NOT ALL WHO SEE, PERCEIVE

The Grand Revelation: When Divinity Showed Its Scale

On the battlefield of Kurukshetra, Arjun stood paralyzed—not from physical weakness but by the emotional weight of fighting his own kin. At this moment of despair, Lord Krishna revealed His **Virat Swaroop**—the Universal Form. Arjun witnessed a boundless cosmic spectacle: countless faces, eyes, arms, and mouths, with entire galaxies cycling through birth and destruction within a single divine body.

This was not merely a display of power—it was a divine confrontation with truth. Arjun realized that death was not the end, and fear of death could not justify abandoning Dharma. The Universe, as Krishna showed, was in constant motion—creation and destruction were its rhythms. Arjun, upon realizing this, surrendered his doubts and picked up his bow—not for glory or revenge, but for duty with clear intent.

The Missed Moment: Duryodhan's Denial of Dharma

Krishna revealed His **Virat Swaroop** not once, but twice—first to Arjun on the battlefield, and earlier in the royal court of Hastinapur, when He made a final, peaceful plea for justice. Duryodhana, however, rejected the appeal and the divine vision alike. Unlike Arjun, who was shaken into awareness, Duryodhana dismissed the cosmic form as mere illusion or trickery. His eyes were open, but his heart was closed.

He was not blind by sight, but by ego. Where Arjun saw a higher truth and surrendered to dharma, Duryodhana clung to pride and power, sealing his path to destruction.

The message is timeless: Divine wisdom reveals itself—but only to those who are willing to see with humility and act with noble intent.

Ignoring the Virat Swaroop: How Modern Leaders Deny Truth and Conscience

The Virat Swaroop was not just a religious spectacle—it is a spiritual metaphor for our times. In the Mahabharat, the moment when Krishna reveals his *Virat Swaroop* to Duryodhana is not merely a spectacle of divine might—it is a profound moral and spiritual revelation. It's truth in its rawest, most awe-inspiring form. Yet Duryodhana, blinded by arrogance, entitlement, and an insatiable hunger for power, scoffs at the revelation. He does not just deny Krishna's cosmic truth—he declares war on it.

Fast forward to the present day, and we are surrounded by modern Duryodhanas. The *Virat Swaroop* today is not a singular divine form—it is truth itself: scientific truth, historical truth, moral clarity, and the collective wisdom of centuries. Yet, like Duryodhana, many modern leaders and influencers mock, suppress, or distort it, fearing what it may reveal about their actions, systems, and greed-fueled agendas.

We see it in corporate greed that denies environmental destruction, in politicians ignoring mass suffering for vote banks, or even in families where personal pride blinds members from doing what's morally right.

Modern examples are plenty:

- World leaders denying humanitarian crisis until irreversible damage is done.
- Tech giants pushing harmful algorithms despite knowing their mental health impact.
- Individuals refusing to change toxic behavior even when shown its consequences.

Truth on Trial

Despite overwhelming scientific evidence on climate change, pandemic risks, vaccine efficacy, and ecological collapse, large sections of political and corporate leadership continue to deny or dilute these truths. Entire machinery is devoted to misinformation—not ignorance, but willful suppression. They ignore the *Virat Swaroop* of science and knowledge because it threatens the empires they've built on exploitation.

Just as Duryodhana dismissed Krishna's divine truth, today's propagandists dismiss climate scientists as alarmists, journalists as liars, and activists as 'woke' radicals. Their strategy is clear: drown out clarity with confusion, flood the moral landscape with so much noise that people stop recognizing truth when they see it.

The Attack on Conscience and Social Awareness

In ancient times, the *Virat Swaroop* struck fear in those with even a shred of humility. Today, conscience itself is under siege. Acts of compassion, inclusion, and justice are labeled as weakness or "wokeness." Human rights are pitted against nationalism. The marginalized are gaslit into silence. Like Duryodhana, modern power brokers fear empathy, because it interferes with their pursuit of dominance.

Social media algorithms amplify anger and outrage while muting reason and reflection. Surveillance capitalism (A system where companies turn personal data into profit by analyzing it to predict and influence human behavior, unlike traditional capitalism which focuses on selling goods and services) commodifies attention, leaving little space for deep thought. Even education is being reshaped—not to liberate minds, but to manufacture conformity. The war on *consciousness* is not collateral—it is the front line.

The Mahabharat war was not inevitable—it became inevitable because Duryodhana refused to see. He saw Krishna, but not the divine. He saw the Pandavas, but not the shared blood

Today, we are at a similar juncture. The *Virat Swaroop* of interconnected crises—climate, inequality, misinformation, hatred—is staring us in the face. If we continue to deny it, or dismiss it, we too risk a modern-day Kurukshetra—one fought not on battlefields, but in classrooms, media houses, hospitals, and parliaments.

The ancient texts warned us—not through superstition but through metaphor. When conscience is ignored and truth is mocked, collapse is not far. The *Virat Swaroop* will not vanish. It will remain, unmoved, waiting for us to open our eyes.

Let us not be Duryodhanas.

Let us be Arjuns—willing to pause, to see, to ask, and ultimately, to act with dharma.

The Virat Swaroop, in essence, appears before us every day—not in divine form, but in the overwhelming truths we ignore.

CHAPTER 24

THE CONCH OF CONSCIENCE: WHEN DUTY RISES, INTENT IS TESTED

The Awakening of Arjun

As Krishna concluded His divine discourse and Arjun shed the last remnants of doubt, the warrior stood up with clarity in his heart and purpose in his grip. He picked up his Gandiva bow, finally ready to fulfill his dharma on the battlefield of Kurukshetra. Fully satisfied that Arjun had overcome his inner conflict, Krishna blew His sacred Panchajanya conch, symbolizing the official start of the Mahabharata war.

This was not just a signal for war—it was the sound of duty awakened, illusions dispelled, and intent aligned with righteousness.

The Call of Conch: Duty vs. Destruction

In response, the great warriors of Kurukshetra blew their conch shells, each symbolizing a unique lineage, purpose, and resolve. The sound of these conches, distinct and commanding, echoed across the battlefield. Yet beneath this ancient ritual lay a deeper truth: while the war raged fiercely, it adhered to a moral code. The battle was fought in open daylight, kept away from civilian areas, and observed rules of engagement—even in its brutality. This was a far cry from the modern nature of warfare.

Today, wars no longer follow such boundaries. Cities are shattered, homes are burned, and innocent lives are uprooted as conflicts spill into populated areas. There are no designated hours for battle, and civilians are no longer shielded from destruction. The very essence of noble intent is lost in the chaos—collateral damage has replaced the conscience that once guided warriors.

The Cost of the First Day

As the sun set on the first day of battle, the Pandavas faced a harsh blow. Uttara and Sweta, the sons of King Virata fell fighting valiantly against the Kaurava forces. Their courage astonished the enemy. Krishna consoled the Pandavas reminding them that they had fulfilled their duty and earned an honorable place in history.

Yet grief lingered. Noble intent does not shield one from pain—but it gives that pain meaning.

Strategy and Setbacks

Arjun knew he could not falter. The next day, he strategized to directly target Bhishma, commander of the Kaurava army. He believed a sudden, bold attack would shake the enemy's confidence and morale. But fate had other plans. Though Krishna drove the chariot straight into battle and Arjun engaged Bhishma in fierce combat, protective formations and divine timing saved Bhishma.

As the saying goes: Man proposes, God disposes.

Arjun did not waver. When the intent is noble, even failure becomes fuel for renewed action—not a reason to give up.

Other Warriors, Other Moments

Elsewhere on the battlefield, Dhrishtadyumna—the son of King Drupada—rushed to rescue Bhima from the fierce assault of Dronacharya, the very teacher who had once humiliated Drupada. This moment carried deep personal history and retribution, echoing the tangled motivations behind the war.

The tide shifted once more when Duryodhana, determined to crush Bhima, deployed the powerful Kalinga army. Their king, Shrutayu—also called Bhanuman—joined forces with Ketumanta, the leader of the Nishadas, to ambush Bhima in a brutal offensive. But retreat was not a concept Bhima entertained. He responded with a relentless barrage of arrows.

Shakradeva, son of the Kalinga King, engaged him head-on—only to be struck down by Bhima's iron mace in a single, ferocious blow that demolished not just the warrior, but also his chariot, charioteer, and horses in one mighty sweep.

In what became one of the most astonishing feats of the war, Bhima climbed up an elephant using its tusks, and in a swift move, stood face-to-face with Bhanuman. In the blink of an eye, Bhima sliced the Kalinga King in half, sealing the fate of the once-feared Kalingas with sheer brute force and unshakable will.

In another surprising twist, Satyaki—the leader of Krishna's Narayani Sena—momentarily set aside his allegiance to the Kauravas. Though pledged to them, he rushed to aid Bhima against Bhishma. It was a moment of moral conflict, where loyalty to dharma briefly overpowered military obligation. This rare defection spoke volumes about the individual struggle between duty and righteousness in the hearts of even seasoned warriors.

Modern Reflections: The Fragile Thread Between Power and Purpose

In today's world, strategies falter, battles are lost, and even the righteous sometimes fall. But the line that separates destruction from transformation is not power—it is intent. Like Arjun, one must rise each day with clarity of purpose, drawing strength from past failures and refusing to abandon dharma. Victory, when rooted in noble intent, endures. In contrast, blind ambition—whether in Duryodhana's stubborn defiance or in the recklessness of modern-day leaders—inevitably leads to ruin, even when cloaked as success.

These inner battles haven't vanished; they have merely changed arenas. In boardrooms, bureaucracies, parliaments, and warzones, individuals still face the dilemma of choosing between allegiance to authority and loyalty to conscience. Like Satyaki, who defied his assigned side for a moment of righteousness, today's whistleblowers speak out, risking careers for truth. Soldiers rescue rather than destroy. Activists challenge power not for gain, but for justice. And like Bhima, some refuse to retreat in the face of injustice, meeting betrayal with renewed purpose instead of despair.

Yet unlike the Mahabharata, where such actions were deeply personal and often guided by an inner code, modern systems tend to reward obedience over integrity, and strategic compliance over moral clarity.

We must ask ourselves: have we truly evolved in how we lead, fight, and serve—or have we simply masked our ethical erosion in polished justifications?

The answer may define whether our age writes its own Mahabharata—or repeats it, stripped of honor.

CHAPTER 25

ACTION WITHOUT INTENT; DUTY WITHOUT DEPTH

The Illusion of Right Action

"*What you think is not important. What you do is.*" – *Mark Twain*

The war had already shattered bodies and hearts when Arjun turned to Krishna—not just as a warrior, but as a man torn between what he felt and what he was supposed to do. The battlefield was no longer just soil stained with blood; it had become a stage for impossible moral decisions. Arjun, weighed down by inner conflict, asked a question that echoes across generations:

"O Janardana! If knowledge is truly higher than action, why do you push me toward this horrific war? Your words seem contradictory. Please tell me clearly—what path leads to the greatest good?"

Krishna's reply wasn't merely about fighting a war—it was about living a life. Through the Gita, he revealed a profound truth that still rings true in today's offices, parliaments, and homes: Action alone means nothing if it lacks intention. It is not the sword, the speech, or the signature that defines righteousness—it is the intent behind the act.

Action for Action's Sake Is Not Dharma

Krishna explained that while quiet contemplation can lead to wisdom, the path of *karma*—action—is inescapable for anyone living in this world. Human beings are driven by their inner tendencies, known as **gunas**—the qualities of nature that shape our behavior. These include **sattva** (clarity and balance), **rajas** (desire and restlessness), and **tamas** (ignorance and inertia). No one is beyond their influence. Even choosing not to act is still a form of action—especially if it stems from fear, pride, or selfish motives.

Krishna warned against the illusion of spiritual superiority—the kind that pretends to renounce worldly life while secretly clinging to desires. True action, he said, is not about outward performance, but inward detachment. When done without craving rewards, action becomes sacred. It becomes a **yagna**—a selfless offering to the divine and to society. This kind of action sustains the world.

But Krishna did not stop there. He sharply criticized those who only take from the world without giving back. "Those who cook and eat for themselves alone are wicked," he said. In other words, those who enjoy the fruits of life without contributing to others or the greater good are thieves in a moral sense. Dharma is not about self-serving success. It is built on service, sacrifice, and responsibility.

Duty Done for Glory Isn't Duty

Krishna reminded Arjun that spiritual liberation does not come from running away from responsibilities. He cited the example of King Janak, who attained enlightenment not by renouncing his duties, but by performing them with detachment and clarity. Janak remained fully engaged in the world, yet unaffected by its outcomes.

Even Krishna Himself—though free from any personal obligation—chose to act. His role was to maintain cosmic order. If He failed to perform His duties, it would set a dangerous example. Chaos would follow.

He explained:

"If I stopped acting, people would follow my example. The world would fall into disorder."

Krishna emphasized that those with wisdom have a quiet responsibility—to guide those who lack understanding. But they must do so gently, without confusing or frightening others. People act according to their innate nature. Trying to force change without compassion or awareness can do more harm than good.

And yet, throughout the Mahabharata, many—from both the Kaurava and Pandava camps—wrapped personal ambition in the language of dharma. Their actions were often driven by ego, pride, or revenge—not the selfless spirit Krishna preached. The Gita was never a call for blind obedience. It was a call for conscious action rooted in noble intent.

That's a truth many warriors then—and leaders today—still fail to grasp.

The Real Enemy: Desire Masquerading as Purpose

Arjun then asked:

"What compels a person to act against their own will?"

Krishna answered: "desire—born of rajas (passion)—which becomes anger when unfulfilled" Like fire, it consumes clarity and spreads ruin. Even the wise fall prey. Lust, ambition, ego—they all cloud intellect and overpower the soul. To overcome this, one must discipline the senses, control the mind, and rise above the impulses.

Krishna spoke about the hierarchy of control: the senses are driven by objects, the mind controls the senses, intellect controls the mind, and the Self (Atman) is above the intellect. To conquer desire, one needs to ascend this hierarchy, ultimately realizing the Self and using it to control the mind, thereby conquering lust and other desires.

To overcome desire, especially destructive ones like lust, greed, or pride, one must ascend this internal ladder. It's not enough to restrain the senses—you must train the mind, sharpen the intellect, and ultimately align with the Self, the silent witness within. Only then can one act with true clarity and control.

Modern Reflections: Action, or Performance?

In today's world, we are drowning in activity—policies passed, deals signed, statements made—but how much of it comes from conscious alignment with higher principles?

The senses chase gratification: scrolling social media, shopping, consuming outrage.

The mind justifies it all: "It's normal," "Everyone does it."

The intellect, if dulled, becomes a servant of ambition.

The Self—the source of wisdom—is rarely consulted.

Think of:

- The bureaucrat who drafts laws that harm the poor to please political masters.
- The executive who champions sustainability while outsourcing labor to sweatshops.
- The politician who performs public gestures of empathy but sidesteps real reform.

They appear dutiful—but their actions are hollow, performed out of habit, ambition, or fear.

They are doing—but not being. Their acts resemble duty, but they lack the soul of dharma: self-awareness, integrity, and sacrifice.

In contrast:

- **Whistleblowers** speak out not for applause, but because they cannot stay silent in the face of injustice. Their courage comes from within.

- **Soldiers**, like Bhima, may respond to betrayal with force—but what makes their actions just or unjust lies in their inner conflict. Is it revenge, or righteousness?

Their alignment of intent and action channels the soul of dharma—purposeful, responsible, and awake.

And yet, our systems reward:

- **Loyalty over truth**
- **Conformity over courage**
- **Optics over ethics**

We have institutions of action, but often hollowed of intent. The soul of dharma is not in what we do—but in why we do it.

The Mahabharata warns us: **Action without intent is noise. Intent without action is silence. Only when the two align does dharma unfold.**

Let the lesson be this:

In a world that idolizes performance, the rarest courage lies in choosing purpose over power and integrity over illusion.

CHAPTER 26

PRECISION AND PURPOSE; WHEN WAR DEMANDS WISDOM

Calculated Fury; The Ethics of Power and Precision

As dawn broke over the blood-soaked fields of Kurukshetra, Arjun took charge restructuring his forces into a crescent—or half-moon—battle formation. This was no symbolic move; it was a calculated, tactical maneuver designed to counter the swelling strength of the Kauravas army. Duryodhana, eager to break through this arc of resistance, hurled ten thousand warriors toward it.

The battlefield ignited into a storm of steel and flesh.

Abhimanyu and Satyaki charged forward like blazing comets, cutting through enemy ranks with unmatched precision. Bhima and his son Ghatotkacha, the formidable half-rakshasa warrior, hurled themselves toward Duryodhana's chariot, shaking its very foundation. So fierce was their attack that Duryodhana's charioteer fled in terror, leaving his master vulnerable and exposed.

Despite these bold advances, the Pandavas paid a steep price. Dronacharya and Bhishma, relentless and revered, launched a furious counterattack. Entire divisions of the Pandavas army were cut down, the ground littered with broken bodies and shattered armor.

As the day wore on and the tide swelled, Arjun found himself encircled. When Arjun was attacked en masse, he invoked the Mahendra Astra—a celestial weapon attributed to Lord Indra.

A divine deluge of arrows poured from the heavens, streaking like fire across the sky. The Mahendra Astra was no ordinary weapon—it was surgical, precise, targeting warriors by intent and merit. Unlike modern weapons of mass destruction that obliterate terrain and civilians alike, this weapon spared the innocent and the environment. And yet, even with such discernment, the sheer scale of the assault was horrific. Kurukshetra ran red, rivers of blood swallowing the footprints of the living.

By sunset, the Pandavas had gained ground—but at an unimaginable cost. Warriors lay strewn across the field. Horses collapsed beside their riders. The air smelled of sweat, ash, and sorrow. Victory was no longer a matter of glory; it came dressed in silence and grief.

Krishna's Dharma Dialogues

And still, in the heart of that chaos, Krishna—the charioteer, philosopher, and divine guide—spoke softly to Arjun. Steering not just the chariot but Arjun's very soul, he offered truths that were sharper than any weapon.

"Understand this," he said, "action alone is not enough. Intent matters. Action without self-awareness is dangerous."

Each day, Krishna unraveled the threads of karma, detachment, and duty—not to numb Arjun's humanity, but to anchor it. He reminded him that desireless action, done as sacrifice, could purify the soul. But without insight, even the most noble of deeds became hollow rituals.

He warned, "Discipline, yoga, and charity—these are fires of transformation. But without understanding, they're like clay lamps in the wind—flickering, aimless."

Only when humility, service, and reflection light the path, Krishna said, does true transformation begin. "Control over the senses leads to wisdom. And wisdom alone brings peace."

Modern-Day Mahendra Astra: Precision with Perils

In the great war of Kurukshetra, Arjun, guided by Krishna, invoked the Mahendra Astra—a weapon of precision and devastating force, unleashed not in fury, but with measured intent. It was aimed at specific enemies, wielded with a code, a dharma that sought to spare the innocent even amid war. Yet, even with divine precision, caution was never abandoned, for the line between victory and unintended destruction was perilously thin.

Today, in the era of drones, PGMs (Precision-Guided Munitions), and satellite-guided missiles, the Mahendra Astra has found its parallel.

Nations tout the advent of precision warfare as a moral evolution in conflict—surgical strikes that promise to eliminate terror cells, neutralize militant infrastructure, and cripple enemy command chains. The 2019 Balakot and Operation Sindoor strikes by India echoed this philosophy—measured, focused, and non-escalatory. No Pakistani military facilities were targeted; the intention was symbolic and strategic: to destroy the machinery of terror, not the state itself.

Yet, modern history is riddled with the Precision Paradox. In Iraq (2003), bombs accurately struck Saddam's hideouts and "Chemical Ali's" residence—but failed to neutralize the intended threats. Worse, they led to over 100 civilian deaths, showing that accuracy without contextual intelligence and ground verification results in "accurate, but ineffective" devastation.

The Afghanistan drone strike in 2021 is another tragic testament. It precisely hit a car suspected of carrying enemy combatants. But among the victims were seven children. This was not an anomaly—it was one among thousands of such errant strikes that challenge the notion of "clean wars".

Much like Arjun in the battlefield, today's military commanders confront a moral dilemma: to strike or not, to rely on machines and real-time data, or wait for confirmation at the risk of losing momentum. The assumption that modern militaries can be dismantled by decisive, surgical hits has proven unrealistic. Wars, as in Ukraine, become attritional, not because of lack of power, but because precision without prudence is impotent.

Russia's missile strikes on civilian centers—maternity hospitals, train stations, apartment complexes illustrate how precision in the wrong hands becomes a tool of terror. PGMs become not Mahendra Astras of restraint, but Kali's unleashed fury, disregarding laws, ethics, and humanity.

India's strategic path must heed these lessons. While the development and deployment of cruise missiles, SRBMs (Short-Range Ballistic Missiles) , loitering munitions (drones or munitions that hover or"loiter" over a target area for some time before diving down to strike), and killer drones are vital for national defense, especially in mountainous terrains and volatile borders—the spirit of Mahendra Astra demands that precision be paired with discernment.

The *Precision Paradox* reminds us: even when weapons hit their mark, if the consequence deepens chaos, they fail in purpose. Just as Arjuna sought Krishna's guidance before releasing divine weapons, modern-day leaders and strategists must anchor technological power within a framework of ethical realism, accountability, and human empathy.

In the end, it's not about how sharp the arrow flies, but why and where it lands.

The future of warfare will depend not on perfect aim alone, but on perfect judgment.For it is not only with swords that we fight, but with choices. And in that, the war continues.

CHAPTER 27

DUTY WITHOUT DESIRE

The Yogi's Discipline: Action Without Attachment

On the blood-stained plains of Kurukshetra, Krishna's voice rose above the chaos—not to teach Arjun how to kill, but how to live.

He spoke of yoga—not as bending the body, but as aligning the mind and soul. True renunciation, he said, lies not in escaping the world, but in performing one's duties without craving the result.

A yogi is not one who runs away to the forest but one who controls the senses while staying in the world. He eats little, sleeps little, speaks less, and listens more. He does not chase reward but focuses on *righteous effort*. He learns to control his mind—because if he doesn't, it becomes his biggest enemy.

He treats success and failure with equal poise, friend and enemy with equal heart. He brings his wandering thoughts back like a shepherd reining in stray sheep. He does not act for applause, nor does he despair in silence. His compass is clear—action rooted in dharma, not desire.

Day Eight: The Battlefield Bleeds

As Krishna concluded this timeless counsel, the war thundered forward into its eighth day. Conches blew, blood flowed, and tempers exploded.

Bhim, ferocious and determined, killed seventeen of Dhritarashtra's sons. Iravan, son of Arjuna and Naga princess Ulupi, was killed by the demon Alambusha on the 8th day of the Kurukshetra war, on the orders of Duryodhana. Alambusha was eventually slain by Bhim.

The day ended with no victory, no peace—just mounting losses. The battlefield remained a stage where duty was performed but intentions remained questionable, tangled in personal vengeance and royal ego.

Modern Echoes: Desireless Devotion in a Desire-Driven World

In today's world, people often chase success, recognition, or profit in everything they do. Students study mainly to get high marks, not always to understand. Employees work hard for promotions, not necessarily for excellence. Even in relationships, people often give with the hope of receiving something back. This focus on results has made work stressful and competitive.

But what if we worked simply for the joy of doing something well?

Imagine someone cooking not to impress anyone, but because they love cooking. The food turns out good naturally because their full attention and love is in the process. Or think of a gardener who grows plants not for selling fruits, but because they enjoy being close to nature. Their joy comes from the act itself, not the result.

There are many people around us who do this. A teacher gives her best even if students may not remember her name. An intern works sincerely without expecting praise, believing the experience itself matters. These are people who act without always thinking, "What will I get from this?" These are modern yogis, warriors of quiet nobility

This kind of work is peaceful and fulfilling. It doesn't carry the stress of "what if I fail?" because success is not the goal—doing the work well is. When we are fully present in what we do, with no hidden agenda or pressure for reward, the work becomes a form of meditation. We feel connected, calm, and more alive.

This is what ancient wisdom like the Bhagavad Gita teaches:

"You have the right to act, but not to the fruits of your actions."

In simple terms, focus on doing your duty with love and honesty. Don't get attached to what you might gain from it. Let the result take care of itself.

Desireless action doesn't mean doing nothing. It means doing everything with full involvement, but without selfish expectations. This way of living brings inner peace, deeper relationships, and true satisfaction—not just for one person, but for everyone around.

So in a world full of chasing and comparing, be the one who plants trees for the next generation, who works with a smile, and who gives their best—just because it's worth doing.

Krishna's message, then and now, reminds us:

कर्मण्येवाधिकारस्ते मा फलेषु कदाचन।

मा कर्मफलहेतुर्भूर्मा ते सङ्गोऽस्त्वकर्मणि॥

You have the right to perform your actions, but not to the fruits thereof.

Do not let the fruits of action be your motive, nor let your attachment be to inaction.

CHAPTER 28

THE TIMELESS WISDOM OF ACHIEVEMENT

Seeking Shelter in the Supreme

Arjun, shaken by the death of his valiant son Iravan, turned to Krishna with a troubled heart. Amidst the chaos of Kurukshetra, his question was simple but profound:

"How does one seek refuge in You?"

What he sought was not escape—but clarity, purpose, and peace.

Krishna, with unshakable calm, replied, "It is simple, Arjun. Fix your mind on Me—not just in thought, but in understanding, in realization of the *Supersoul*. Through the path of purification and disciplined knowledge, some rare souls, after many births come to know Me in truth."

He continued:

"Earth, water, fire, air, and ether—these five elements form the foundation of all existence. To this, human beings are gifted with three more: mind, intellect, and ego. These eight constitute My material energy. But beyond these lies My supreme energy—the *soul*, the spark of life, subtle and eternal."

Krishna wasn't merely listing cosmic laws. He was painting a portrait of divine interconnectedness. "I am the taste in water, the light in the sun and moon, the sacred syllable *Om* in the Vedas, the heat in fire, the fragrance in earth. Where discipline resides in ascetics and strength in the selfless— there too, I am."

The *Supersoul*, He said, dwells in all beings. The wise recognize Me in their wisdom. Those who act without lust or craving, with detached virtue, are always near Me—even without temples or rituals.

The Four Paths and Their Fates

Krishna described four types of seekers:

1. **The Distressed**: Seek divine help in times of suffering.
2. **The Seeker of Knowledge**: Pursue truth and understanding of the self and divine.
3. **The Seeker of Material Gain**: Turn to the divine for wealth and success.
4. **The Wise, Devoted Soul**: Know the Absolute and serve with pure, unwavering devotion.

Krishna cherished them all, but the wise—the one who seeks Him for His own sake—He called *"the very Self of My Self."* Such souls, even if it takes lifetimes, rise beyond delusion and find liberation. Those who chase lesser deities may get fleeting blessings, but those who reach for the eternal are never reborn in ignorance.

Transcendence Amidst Bloodshed

As the war waged on, Arjun saw his kin fall one by one. The grief that once nearly paralyzed him at the war's start resurfaced in waves. Krishna, however, stayed ahead of that emotional tide—feeding Arjun's mind with transcendental wisdom, so it would not be drowned by guilt or attachment.

Virtuous deeds elevate; impure ones degrade. But in this erratic world, ruled by unpredictable turns of time and emotion, only one thing anchors the soul—noble intent. Krishna knew Arjun's heart was noble but wavering. So He anchored it with eternal truths.

True transcendence, Krishna said, isn't only found in scriptures or temples. It can bloom in a silent forest, in the whisper of leaves, in the dissolving ego that listens to the symphony of nature. Even music can lead to the divine, if it moves your soul, not just your ears.

Achievement and Anxiety: Krishna's Message for Today's Youth

In the heart of a fierce battlefield, Arjun's heart broke—not just from war, but from the loss of his son, Iravan. In that moment of pain, he turned to Krishna looking for clarity.

Today's youth, too, stand on their own battlefield—one of pressure, comparison, and constant expectation. The modern world celebrates achievement—marks, medals, degrees, fame. But in chasing these, many young people lose their sense of peace. Behind perfect Instagram posts and glowing report cards, there are growing levels of anxiety, burnout, and emptiness.

Surveys show that most young people today value personal success over compassion or community. They're told from an early age that to be successful, they must always be the best—top of the class, leader of the club, star of the team. In this environment, perfectionism isn't a rare trait, it's the norm. And it's taking a toll on their mental health.

But where do they learn this? From adults.

We model a life of endless striving. We say we want our children to be kind, balanced, and joyful but our actions tell them otherwise. We applaud achievements more than we acknowledge effort or empathy. We chase success in our own lives, setting a silent example that worth is tied to results.

This way of living creates a cycle—one that leaves us exhausted and our children anxious.

And yet, ancient wisdom still offers a way out.

Krishna's message to Arjun was simple but powerful: do your duty, but let go of the attachment to the outcome. Achievement is not wrong—but obsession with results is. True strength lies not in controlling what happens, but in how we act, how we serve, and how we connect with something higher than ourselves.

In today's world, this could mean redefining success—not as being better than others, but as making a positive difference. Not as collecting trophies, but as growing into a person of character, humility, and purpose.

Instead of asking children, *"What did you score?"*—we could ask, *"What did you learn?"*

Instead of, *"Did you win?"*—we could ask, *"Did you enjoy doing your best?"*

Achievement, when driven by ego, isolates us. But when it comes from a place of service and purpose, it connects us with others, and with ourselves.

Like Arjun, we may face battles that shake us. But Krishna's timeless wisdom reminds us: when we seek shelter not in results, but in right action and inner steadiness, peace will follow. It's not the absence of ambition but the presence of meaning that makes all the difference.

Let us teach our youth that the highest form of success is not in climbing over others, but in lifting others along the way. That in the noise of competition, the quiet voice of the soul still matters. And that even in a fast-moving world, the stillness of purpose is a shelter worth seeking—**for it is not how far you run, but why you run, that defines the journey.**

CHAPTER 29

THE STRATEGIC SILENCE: SHIKHANDI AND THE MORAL BLIND SPOT

The Battlefield Dilemma

On the ninth day of the war, Bhishma, the Kaurava commander, was disheartened. Despite leading a massive army, the desired breakthrough remained elusive. In desperation, he began an aggressive onslaught, causing immense damage to the Pandava forces. Krishna, witnessing the carnage and Arjun's hesitance, drove the chariot head-on toward Bhishma, hoping to stir Arjun into action.

But Arjun, bound by his deep reverence for Bhishma, restrained his arrows. His mind was clouded—not by fear, but by familial emotion. Bhishma's arrows were merciless; Arjun's resolve, however, was soft. Enraged, Krishna descended from the chariot, lifting a broken wheel like a weapon, rushing at Bhishma. The scene stunned the battlefield: the divine breaking His promise not to bear arms. Krishna had declared he would not pick up arms during the war. Bhishma, knowing Krishna's deep love for dharma and his emotional ties with the Pandavas, sought to provoke him into breaking his word.

Bhishma welcomed death at Krishna's hands. But Arjun intervened, pleading for restraint. "You promised," he said, falling at Krishna's feet. Krishna relented, returning to the chariot but not without sorrow and rage on His face.

An Unlikely Shield: The Deployment of Shikhandi

On the tenth day of the Kurukshetra war, Bhishma, the undefeatable warrior, continued to devastate the Pandava army. His valor and skill were unmatched, and it became evident to Krishna that Bhishma had to fall if the Pandavas were to stand any chance of victory. But the dilemma was deeper than just strategy—it was emotional. How could Arjun, bound by respect for his grandsire, ever raise his bow against him?

Then emerged a bold and unconventional solution: the deployment of Shikhandi.

Shikhandi was born without male or female organs—a Kinnar. In those times, such children were often cast away by families and raised in transgender communities that lived on the fringes of society. These communities were bound by religious taboo: they could not be harmed, yet they were never fully accepted. They survived by performing blessings during births and weddings, their presence considered both auspicious and otherworldly.

But on the battlefield of Kurukshetra, Shikhandi—once an outcast—became a decisive force in changing the course of the war.

Bhishma, who had taken a lifelong vow never to raise weapons against a woman or anyone with feminine identity, saw Shikhandi and instantly lowered his bow. That moment of restraint was all Arjun needed.

Standing behind Shikhandi, Arjun unleashed a relentless volley of arrows. Bhishma did not retaliate. He fell—pierced, yet dignified in his silence.

Thus, the very individual society once rejected became the key to defeating its most revered warrior. A child discarded at birth ended up shaping the course of an epic war.

Modern-Day Shikhandi: Revered When Useful, Reviled When Not

In the epic Mahabharata, Shikhandi's journey is both powerful and painful. The story of Shikhandi holds a mirror to society's long-standing hypocrisy. Those born different are often denied dignity, compassion, and even the right to exist equally. Yet, when convenient, the same society does not hesitate to place them at the center of its own survival. Shikhandi was born Shikhandini, assigned female at birth and later identified as male. His transformation—from a rejected child to a warrior—is not just a tale of personal identity, but one of society's selective morality. Shikhandi was abandoned at birth, denied both parental love and societal inclusion. Yet on the battlefield, the very identity for which he was shunned suddenly made him a tactical asset.

Shikhandi was never truly accepted. And yet, when war demanded strategy over ethics, when Bhishma—a warrior bound by a vow never to fight a woman—needed to be defeated, Shikhandi was brought forward. Not as a respected warrior, but as a body to hide behind. A tool to exploit. Shikhandi, who was denied dignity, suddenly became indispensable.

Fast forward to modern India. The parallels are painful.

The transgender community often called hijras—has existed in the subcontinent for centuries. In ancient times, they held positions of respect, especially in Mughal courts, where they served as trusted guards and advisors. In Hindu mythology, they were bestowed divine status. According to the Ramayana, when Lord Rama returned from exile, he found the hijras waiting loyally at the edge of the forest, having refused his command to return. Moved by their devotion, he blessed them with the power to confer blessings and curses.

But this reverence coexisted with deep-rooted stigma. In 1871, during British colonial rule, the Criminal Tribes Act labeled hijras as "habitual offenders," criminalizing their very existence. This branding carried into post-independence India, where they continued to be treated as pariahs—begging at signals, excluded from mainstream jobs, and mocked in public discourse. The social ostracism was total; economic opportunity, almost non-existent.

A turning point came in 2014, when the Supreme Court of India recognized transgender individuals as the "third gender" in the landmark *NALSA vs. Union of India* judgment. This decision acknowledged their constitutional rights and ordered governments to provide reservations, welfare schemes, and protection against discrimination. The Transgender Persons (Protection of Rights) Act, passed in 2019, further codified these rights, though it received criticism from the community for its top-down approach and lack of self-identification rights.

Despite these legal advancements, the lived reality of most transgender individuals remains one of exclusion and tokenism.They face systemic exclusion. Many are disowned by their families, barred from education, pushed out of employment, and denied healthcare. They are mocked on streets, harassed by authorities, and treated as second-class citizens in a society that preaches inclusivity but practices indifference.

And yet, during weddings and childbirths, they are invited to bless the event. Corporations parade them during Pride Month not for meaningful inclusion, but for corporate optics. They are offered political tickets—not as leaders, but as symbols. Films showcase them to evoke sympathy, yet rarely hand them narratives with dignity. Panels showcase them to appear progressive. Society continues to applaud their "resilience" while denying them everyday respect.

They are still the Shikhandis of our time—called upon when needed, erased when not. When they serve a purpose—cultural, commercial, or political—they are welcomed. Once that purpose is fulfilled, they are forgotten, discarded, or pushed back to the margins.

Like Shikhandi, today's transgender individuals are often respected only in moments of convenience and strategy, not as human beings with dignity, agency, and rights. They are turned into metaphors and myths, not citizens.

The law may now recognize them as the "third gender," but society still struggles to accept them as equals. And so, the question remains: has much changed since Shikhandi stood on the battlefield?

From Kurukshetra to the Constitution, Shikhandi's body remains a shield—wielded by a society that exploits without empathy. It's time we stop hiding behind them, and finally stand with them.

The Mahabharata, through this chilling episode, reminds us not only of moral failures on the battlefield but also the deeper ethical bankruptcy of a civilization that uses what it cannot respect.

When strategy overshadows virtue, and the marginalized become mere tools of convenience, we must ask—not just who won, but what was lost.

CHAPTER 30

THE SILENCE OF LOYALTY: THE COST OF NEUTRALITY

The Super Soul and the Final Release

Arjuna, bewildered by the mysteries of life and death, questioned Krishna about the *Supersoul*—its role, its presence, and its destination after death. Krishna responded with a serene clarity and deep insight:

"The **Adhyatma (अध्यात्म)** is the individual soul—the inner self, eternal and indestructible. It is the consciousness that defines who we are. The **Adhibhuta (अधिभूत)** refers to the material world—the physical nature around us, made of perishable elements that constantly change and evolve. The **Adhidaiva (अधिदैव)** are the divine forces—the deities like the Sun and Moon who govern natural laws, though even they are not eternal. And I am the **Adhiyajna (अधियज्ञ)**—the Supreme Being present in every act of sacrifice. I remain unchanged, accepting all offerings, guiding all actions, and existing beyond time and matter."

Krishna urged that liberation lies in focused devotion. The yogi, disciplined in mind and detached from desire, remembers the Supreme even at the brink of death—chanting *Om*, visualizing the radiant, formless divine. Only then does the soul reach the realm of no return.

Krishna explained the cosmic timing: those who pass away during the bright fortnight ascend; those who depart during the dark return. It's not superstition, but cosmic alignment—an ancient awareness of time's influence on transition.

Two cosmic pathways await the departing soul:

- One, through the bright lunar fortnight (*Uttarayan*), grants liberation.
- The other, through the dark fortnight (*Dakshinayan*), ensures rebirth.

This profound spiritual discourse occurred even as bloodshed and tactical warfare continued on the ninth day of battle.

The Fall of a Giant

On this pivotal day, the Pandavas placed Shikhandi—the only transgender warrior—at the front of their formation. Arjun, shielded behind Shikhandi, attacked Bhishma, knowing that he would not raise weapons against someone he once saw as a woman.

Arrows rained from Arjun's bow—not driven by hatred or personal vendetta, but by the burden of dharma. Though Bhishma was his beloved grandsire and mentor, Arjun knew that righteousness demanded action. In that moment, it was not emotion but duty that guided his hand—a painful, necessary act to restore justice in a world torn by adharma.Bhishma's body did not fall to the ground. Instead, it lay suspended mid-air, pierced by Arjun's shafts—a fitting bed for a warrior who had lived by vows, not comforts.

As a mark of respect, both armies ceased fighting. Arjun gave Bhishma a pillow of arrows. When Bhishma expressed thirst, Arjun fired an arrow into the earth, summoning a stream of cool water to quench him. It was not magic—it was wisdom. Arjuna understood the battlefield's topography, perhaps much like a modern-day hydrogeologist who can read land and locate underground reserves. Today, such groundwater knowledge is buried beneath over-extraction and reckless planning—just as ancient wisdom is lost in the noise of our times.

A Long Wait for the Right Moment

Bhishma chose not to die immediately. He lay there, counting days on his bed of pain, awaiting the celestial alignment of *Uttarayan*—a period deemed auspicious for the soul's final departure. For 88 days, he lingered between life and death.

But why did such a wise and noble man suffer so?

Bhishma had lived by a personal code of duty—but sometimes, duty without timely action becomes complicity. When Draupadi was disrobed in court, Bhishma—the most senior, respected elder—remained silent. His wisdom did not translate into intervention. His strength did not come to her defense. Even Jatayu, a dying bird, fought Ravan to protect Sita. Bhishma, a warrior, chose to uphold allegiance over justice.

Was this delay in his final release a cosmic commentary on his moral inaction?

Perhaps it was the universe's quiet verdict: even the wisest must answer for the silence that condones wrong.

Modern Reflection: The Curse of Institutional Silence

In an empire not very far from ours, the emperor walked proudly through the streets—completely naked. Everyone saw it. His advisors, ministers, generals, even children. But no one said a word.

Some praised the brilliance of his taste.

Others averted their eyes and smiled.

A few dared to look puzzled—but quickly recovered.

The emperor mistook their silence for admiration. Those who frowned were dismissed as troublemakers. He believed he was adorned in robes of wisdom and strength, even as he stood exposed.

This isn't just a fairy tale. It's the reality of every institution, organization, and nation where truth is suppressed and silence is rewarded

And in this silence, Bhishma lives on.

Modern-Day Bhishma: Respected, Wise... and Silent

Bhishma, the elder statesman of the Mahabharata, was bound not by chains, but by a vow.

He knew the war was unjust.

He foresaw the destruction.

He witnessed Draupadi's humiliation.

Yet he stood still—respected, revered, but tragically neutral.

Today, in boardrooms and bureaucracies, courtrooms and classrooms, modern-day Bhishmas observe wrongs, but stay silent. It's not ignorance that weakens modern institutions—it's the silence of those who know better

- Employees who see toxicity but fear backlash.
- Leaders who ignore dissent to preserve hierarchy.
- Judges who follow the letter but not the spirit of the law while justice cries in the shadows.
- Teachers who spot injustice but never raise their voice.
- The bureaucrat who watches policies wreck lives but shields himself behind regulations.
- The academician who critiques the system from a distance but never corrects it.
- The officer who follows orders, even when they trample the very people he swore to protect.

They are not evil.

They are experienced.

They are decorated.

They are afraid.... and tragically neutral.

Like Bhishma, they confuse loyalty for virtue and silence for wisdom. They are bound not by chains, but by the fear of consequence.

And the battlefield? It isn't Kurukshetra—it's wherever conscience is pitted against compliance.

And the arrows? Not iron-tipped, but sharp nonetheless.

And so, institutions rot while their wise remain mute—watching, knowing, never intervening.

Behind closed doors, the truth is whispered. On official platforms, praise is bestowed.

Emails remain unsent. Feedback goes unspoken. Problems become rumors. Whistleblowers are branded disloyal.

This is not just a management flaw—it is a moral failing.

So what is the cost of silence?

When people are punished for telling the truth, they stop speaking.

When systems reward compliance over conscience, they stagnate.

When leaders reject criticism, they stand naked—while everyone claps.

Bhishma's silence did not protect Hastinapur. It hastened its downfall.

In our time, organizational silence is no less deadly. It blocks learning, halts reform, and suffocates the brave.

The question is not whether we have Bhishmas among us. We do.

The real question is – will they rise from their silence, or die on a bed of invisible arrows?

Until then, the emperor will remain naked.

And the kingdom, blind.

CHAPTER 31

THE PRICE OF CHOSEN IMMORTALITY

Bhishma and the Burden of Choice

Bhishma Pitamah—once the unshakable pillar of Hastinapur—now lay motionless, not on a bed of comfort, but on a bed of arrows. His fall did not bring instant death. Instead, it led to a prolonged state of waiting—a consequence of the boon of *Iccha Mrityu* (death at will), granted by his father, King Shantanu. In return, Bhishma had taken a lifelong vow of celibacy and loyalty to the throne, committing himself to serve Hastinapur without ever claiming it.

What was meant to be a divine blessing turned into a silent pain. As he lay pierced but breathing, it became clear: his body was broken, but the weight of his conscience was far heavier. Throughout his life, Bhishma followed the letter of dharma but not its spirit. He obeyed orders, served unworthy rulers, and remained silent during Draupadi's humiliation. His silence was not noble restraint—it was moral failure.

And so, Bhishma lingered—trapped between life and death—on a battlefield that did not just reveal the cruelty of the Kauravas, but also the quiet complicity of elders who knew better, yet chose to do nothing.

The Divine Unseen: Krishna's Path to True Understanding

To clarify Arjun's doubts about duty and existence, Krishna revealed the deeper truth of life and the cosmos. He explained, "At the end of each cosmic cycle, all beings return to Me, and at the beginning of the next, I send them forth. Though I engage in actions, I remain untouched by them. While fools mock My form, the wise see Me in every offering, in every sacred syllable, and in every act of love. They do not simply study the scriptures—they live by them. They do not worship out of fear, but surrender with love. Through their devotion, they are freed from the cycle of karma and rebirth, returning to Me."

In this, Krishna emphasized the difference between ritualistic actions and actions performed for deeper spiritual realization. He distinguished between the learned and the wise, highlighting the contrast between Bhishma's passive silence and Arjun's active struggle with moral confusion.

When Position Outlives Purpose: The Modern Trap of Staying Too Long

In today's world, the power of *Iccha Mrityu*—the ability to delay one's end—has transformed into a modern dilemma.

Bhishma, the grand patriarch of the Mahabharata, was not truly defeated by Arjuna's arrows, but by the burden of *Iccha Mrityu*—the power to choose his own death. Bound by vows and a sense of duty, he stayed too long. And in that choice, he bore the pain of hundreds of arrows piercing his body, stretched across a bed of agony—not just physical, but the torment of watching a war he could no longer stop, and a kingdom he could no longer guide.

His prolonged presence, once seen as the pillar of wisdom and strength, became a painful reminder of how holding on too long can paralyze action and progress. The arrows didn't kill him—but neither did they let him heal. He lay suspended—between relevance and redundancy, between authority and helplessness.

In today's world, the power of *Iccha Mrityu* shows up differently. It resides in institutions where senior leaders overstay not because they are needed, but because they fear irrelevance. Consider the seasoned executive who once revolutionized an organization, now paralyzed by the fear of becoming irrelevant. Files gather dust on their desk, not out of laziness, but because each decision feels like a potential misstep. Or the senior academic who continues to deliver the same lectures from decades ago, unwilling to let younger voices introduce fresh perspectives. Their influence lingers—not empowering, but eclipsing. In bureaucrats who delay decisions out of caution, mistaking inaction for prudence. In corporate offices where innovation is stalled because the old guard won't relinquish control. The political office where a leader stays "for stability," but breeds stagnation.

They too lie on their own metaphorical bed of arrows—not visibly bleeding, but blocking the system from breathing.

In families, the Bhishma syndrome is evident in patriarchs and matriarchs who continue to wield moral authority long after they have ceased to take moral action. Their silence and control, once protective, now stifle the generations waiting for a voice, a turn, a chance to lead.

Like a driver refusing to adjust their mirrors, they speed ahead unaware of the blind spots: the stifled successors, the deferred reforms, the unspoken frustrations. They wave their signal—intentions clear—but ignore the horns blaring around them. Instead of reflection, there is reaction. Instead of mentoring, there is micromanagement.

In the language of **John Maxwell's Law of the Rubber Band**, they've lost their stretch. And without that tension between what they are and what they could still become, they grow brittle, inert.

This is about self-awareness. About recognizing when your presence helps and when it hinders. It's about understanding when your purpose has served its time. Staying too long, even out of duty, can become its own form of selfishness—one that punishes not just the self, but those waiting in the wings.Bhishma had the power to choose his time of death, but not the wisdom to choose his moment of exit from relevance.

Bhishma's bed of arrows is a haunting metaphor for what happens when leadership becomes a burden instead of a service, and when stepping aside is seen not as surrender, but as wisdom.

The true tragedy? When one's sense of duty becomes a justification for overstaying.

When those in power hold on too long, they cease to be guiding lights and start casting shadows—blocking progress, stifling renewal. True legacy lies not in how long we stay, but in knowing when to step aside.

CHAPTER 32

WHEN COMMAND PASSES WITHOUT CONSCIENCE

After Bhishma's Fall: A Strategic Succession

With Bhishma lying pierced and helpless on the bed of arrows, the Kaurava army stood leaderless at a critical juncture. This could have been a moment for moral reckoning—a pause to reflect on the true cost of the war. Instead, it became a race to fill the vacuum and resume the violence.

Karna, long kept out of the battlefield due to Bhishma's disapproval, saw this as his opening. He approached the dying patriarch— to seek his blessings and legitimize his presence in the war. There was no room for sentiment—only strategy.

Understanding that the army needed a tactician more than a hero, Karna advised Duryodhan to appoint Dronacharya as the next Commander-in-Chief. Though Karna himself was powerful, he acknowledged Drona's authority and battlefield acumen. Duryodhan agreed, and the command passed to a teacher revered for his intellect—but whose sense of right and wrong would soon be put to test.He was a man known for his wisdom and learning—but even greater was his attachment to duty without discernment.

From Righteousness to Strategy

Duryodhan's objective had shifted. It was no longer just about defeating the Pandavas; now, his aim was to end the war quickly by capturing Yudhishthir alive. Dronacharya agreed to this plan, but with one crucial condition: Arjun had to be kept away from the battlefield. What should have raised concerns about fairness and dharma quickly became a tactical move.

A spy overheard this conversation but misunderstood it as a plot to kill Arjun. Alarmed, Yudhishthir quickly warned his brother of the perceived threat. Arjun, with unwavering confidence, responded, "Even if Vishnu himself attacks with all the gods, they cannot harm me."

This was not humility—it was hubris. The war, once fought to uphold righteousness, had now become a battle to protect pride and egos.

War Without Reverence: The Collapse of Duty and Wisdom

Dronacharya, once a paragon of wisdom and spiritual learning, had become a weapon of destruction. The same guru who had imparted knowledge and discipline to both the Kauravas and Pandavas now invoked celestial weapons against the kingdom he had nurtured. His attacks decimated the Panchal forces and forced Dhrishtadyumna, the very warrior destined to slay him, to retreat.

As Arjun faced his old teacher in battle, a deep moral conflict consumed him. Bound by the sacred bond of guru and disciple, he could not bring himself to strike Dronacharya down. How could a pupil, who had been taught to revere his guru as a divine figure, kill the very man who had shaped his understanding of life and combat? Arjun fought with a hesitation that spoke volumes about the weight of tradition and reverence—codes that had long defined honor but now shackled the truth.

The paradox in the Mahabharata lies in the fact that the warriors, by adhering to outdated codes of duty, ended up enabling the very destruction they sought to avoid. On one hand, they fought to uphold dharma (righteousness), but on the other, their strict loyalty to traditional ideals prevented them from taking the necessary actions to end the war or make moral decisions. The two conflicting elements—the desire to uphold righteousness and the failure to adapt to changing realities—created a situation where their very adherence to duty fueled the chaos and destruction.

Across the battlefield, the scene was no different. Shakuni clashed with Sahadeva, Bhima battled Vivinsati, one of the Kaurava brothers, and Nakul forced Shalya to retreat. Friends became foes, and teachers—once respected for their wisdom—now became agents of destruction. The grand conflict, no longer a war of righteousness, had turned into a chaotic struggle, where tradition and outdated codes of duty clouded the path to true wisdom.

Abhimanyu's Stand: Honour Over Glory in a War of Ruins

Abhimanyu, though young and inexperienced compared to the seasoned warriors on the battlefield, emerged as a fierce force to be reckoned with. He fought not for personal glory, but to safeguard the values that the elders had failed to protect. He dragged opponents into defeat, overpowered Jayadrath, and left even the great Dronacharya astounded by his skills. His courage and sense of honor stood in stark contrast to the moral decay around him.

While Abhimanyu rose as a beacon of youthful resolve, the Kaurava army, despite its strength and strategic leadership, began to crumble under the weight of its leaders' ambition and flawed decisions. The war, once fought for a noble cause, now seemed to lose its purpose, as the older generation's mistakes were exposed by the bravery of the young warrior.

Yudhishthir's Strategic Brilliance: Leading with Purpose Amid Chaos

Yudhishthir, often dismissed for his calm demeanor, revealed his true leadership when it mattered most. He displayed sharp strategic insight, orchestrating coordinated attacks that saw Virat, Drupad, Satyaki, Dhrishtadyumna, and others surrounding Dronacharya, cutting through the Kaurava forces with precision. The battlefield became a grim sight, with a river of blood flowing—not just from fallen soldiers, but from the collapse of once-held ideals.

Dronacharya, the revered teacher, had transformed into a mere tool of the Kaurava's cause. In his unwavering loyalty to the throne, he had betrayed the very principles of honor and duty he had once instilled in his disciples.

Modern Reflection: The Risk of Leadership Without Inner Voice

In the Mahabharata, the fall of Bhishma was not just a tactical loss. It was a moral collapse. The Kaurava army, despite its strength, discipline, and numbers, was suddenly adrift. Their tallest pillar, who had long held the illusion of stability, now lay immobilized—his body pierced by arrows, and his wisdom, once revered, rendered impotent. With Bhishma gone, there was strategy, but no soul. Commanders followed, but conviction faltered. The war, once cloaked in dharma, lost its center of gravity.

The army did not collapse because it lacked warriors. It collapsed because it lacked conscience.

Cut to the 21st century. In a glass building, a CEO fires 900 employees over a three-minute Zoom call. No warning, no empathy—just efficiency. The company survives, but something vital dies. A similar hollowness echoes here—the kind that sets in when leadership is severed from its moral compass.

We're witnessing a modern Kaurava moment. Decisions are being made. Plans are being executed. But the purpose? The people? Often ignored.

Competence Without Conscience

Today's organizations often confuse continuity with leadership. The next in line is not always the right one—merely the available one. A leader retires, and another steps in—not to transform, but to protect the status quo. The system demands continuity, so someone must step in.

Imagine a CEO replacing a retiring mentor—not to evolve the company's culture, but to protect the very flaws the predecessor left behind. Or a principal, who takes charge of a crumbling school, yet mirrors the same outdated rules instead of reforming the structure. The chain of command continues, but the spirit weakens. The baton passes, but the deeper issues remain untouched.

Just like Dronacharya, who picked up the mantle after Bhishma—not to question the cause, but to continue the fight. Even when it had lost its moral mandate.

Modern leaders, too, may continue institutions without questioning their purpose. They become enforcers of outdated norms, defenders of flawed systems, guardians of past mistakes.

Leadership without conscience is leadership that performs, but does not reflect. That delivers, but does not heal. That wins quarterly battles, but loses long-term wars.

The Need for Conscious Leadership

In times of global volatility, social tension, and fragile trust, we need leaders who don't just know the numbers, but know the weight of their decisions. Who ask not just *What's in it for me?* but *What's right for all?*

Conscious leadership is not soft leadership. It is leadership with spine and soul. It means leading with empathy, with awareness of the human cost, and with the humility to pause before action.

The most powerful leaders of today won't be those with the loudest voices or the strongest resumes. They'll be those who are willing to say, *I will not shoot another arrow until I know why I'm aiming.*

Legacy and Accountability

Bhishma lay on the bed of arrows by his own will—but also because of his own silence. His refusal to intervene when adharma first took root ultimately paralyzed him. Modern leaders, too, face this dilemma. Will they use their voice when things begin to rot or wait until they are forced to fall?

In both the epic and the era, the message is the same: Power without reflection, leadership without conscience—is a war already lost.

In life, as in the Mahabharata, it is not enough to take charge. One must lead with conscience, or risk becoming a celebrated destroyer.

CHAPTER 33

THE MANIFESTATION OF THE SUPERSOUL

Revealing Divinity: Krishna as the Source of All

On the battlefield of Kurukshetra, amidst war cries and the pounding of chariots, Krishna unveiled a truth that transcends time: "*Sarva Bhutānām Bījam – I am the seed of all beings.*" This wasn't a declaration of supremacy, but an invitation to awaken. In this pivotal moment, Krishna revealed the truth of his divine presence within all—an inner divinity that is the source and sustenance of existence.

He described himself not as an external deity demanding worship, but as the Supersoul—the eternal consciousness residing in every being. His presence is the origin of wisdom, truth, self-restraint, forgiveness, nonviolence, and joy. The great sages, both ancient and present, emerged from his cosmic will. Even gods and demons remain unaware of his true origin, for Krishna is birthless, timeless, and sinless—beyond form yet the source of all forms.

The Cosmic Catalogue: Krishna's Many Manifestations

Responding to Arjun's request for deeper understanding, Krishna enumerated his manifestations: He is the sacred syllable *OM*, the essence of Vedas, the intelligence in the wise, the power in the strong, and the life force in all beings. In nature, he is the Himalayas, the Ganges, the sun, and the moon. Among beings, he manifests as Indra, Rudra, Kubera, and sages like Narada and Vyasa.

Krishna is the seed of all existence—the spark within cows, elephants, and serpents alike. He lives through feminine virtues: fame, speech, memory, intellect, patience, and endurance. Wherever there is beauty, strength, or brilliance, it is but a fraction of his radiant power. He is life and death, the beginning and the end, the destroyer of illusion and the enlightener of souls.

The Forgotten Path: From Wisdom to Mechanical Rituals

What Krishna offered Arjun was more than a theological discourse. It was a shift from transactional faith to transformational realization. He did not speak of hollow rituals, but of awakening—an inward turning to recognize the Supersoul that flickers like a lamp within us, dispelling darkness and doubt. Yet, in the Mahabharata's narrative—and often in our own lives—this realization is buried under ambition, pride, and blind allegiance.

Many of the epic's warriors fought with valor but without awareness. They upheld their roles, mastered weapons, and quoted scriptures—but missed the deeper call to *conscious action*. They served thrones, not truths; victories, not virtues.

Modern Echoes: Leadership Without Light

In today's world, Krishna's divine message holds relevance. We live in an age of astonishing intellect and influence where knowledge abounds, but wisdom often hides. Consider a scientist who pushes the boundaries of innovation but loses sight of ethics. A judge who rules by the book yet suppresses justice. A social leader whose activism is loud, but hollow in compassion. These are modern warriors—high on competence, but dim in conscience.

We admire brilliance, yet forget to ask:

What inner light does it serve?

As Krishna reminded Arjun, true power lies not in possession—but in purpose. Leadership must be lit from within.

When the Light is Absent: Hitler's Rise

Take the rise of Adolf Hitler in Nazi Germany. Charismatic, calculated, and commanding, he transformed a nation into a war machine. But his power was guided by a dark inner void—rooted in fear, hatred, and ego.

Under his leadership, obedience replaced conscience. Millions followed, not because their souls agreed, but because their fears complied. Institutions thrived in structure but rotted in spirit. The legal system legalized oppression. The army executed atrocities.

This was leadership without light—a nation led not by the Supersoul, but by the shadows of unchecked ambition.

Just as Duryodhan rejected Krishna's counsel, Hitler dismissed the soul's voice. The cost: a world torn by war, and generations scarred by silence.

When the Light Leads: Mandela's Example

In contrast, consider Nelson Mandela. After 27 years of imprisonment, he emerged not with vengeance, but with vision. He did not just demand justice – he offered forgiveness. He did not just unite a country – he healed a nation.

His leadership was not transactional – it was transformational. It was rooted in *ubuntu*, the African belief in shared humanity. That is what made him more than a statesman. He was a manifestation of the Supersoul in public life.

Like Krishna guiding Arjun, Mandela led with clarity, humility, and the courage to uphold dharma even when it hurt. He didn't just win freedom; he preserved dignity.

The Divine Spark in Everyday Roles

The Supersoul is not reserved for avatars or saints. It reveals itself in quiet choices:

- A teacher who awakens the inner strength of a student reflects Krishna's light.
- A doctor who heals without ego mirrors divine purpose.
- A leader who serves not systems, but souls, channels the Supreme Teacher within.

These individuals do not need to declare their faith—they embody it.

The Supreme Teacher Within

Krishna's revelation on the battlefield was not meant for Arjun alone. It was meant for all who stand at life's crossroads—of action and awareness, of duty and doubt.

The Mahabharata reminds us: Institutions may stand tall, but without inner awakening, they remain monuments without meaning.

The Supersoul does not scream—it whispers. It does not conquer—it awakens.

May we learn to listen.

In life—as in the Mahabharata—it is not enough to act. One must act with awareness of the divine within, or risk becoming powerful shadows with no light.

CHAPTER 34

FORGIVENESS: AN ATTITUDE OF THE STRONG

The Bitter Harvest of Unforgiveness

The lifelong enmity between Arjun and Duryodhana, rooted in pride and a refusal to forgive, culminated in an unimaginable destruction that wiped out almost the entire Kaurava lineage. Forgiveness, the invisible armor of the strong, was absent. Without it, the battlefield of Kurukshetra became a stage for annihilation rather than reconciliation.

On the twelfth day of the war, Dronacharya, commander of the Kaurava army, obsessed over capturing Yudhishthira alive. He knew that as long as Arjuna stood in the battlefield, this goal was impossible. No army, no matter how vast, could match the focused strength of one determined soul grounded in faith and righteousness.

To outwit Arjun, Dronacharaya plotted a deceitful strategy, violating the noble rules of warfare by continuing battle beyond sunset. He instructed Susharma, a skilled ally, to distract Arjun and lure him away from the battlefield, thus creating an opportunity to ensnare Yudhishthira.

Satyaki's Valor: The Power of Loyalty and Steadiness

While Arjun was engaged elsewhere, Satyaki emerged as the steadfast protector of Yudhishthira. With unwavering loyalty and an unshaken mind, Satyaki defended the Pandava king against the onslaught of the Trigarta forces. Trigarta kingdom, ruled by King Susharma, was a significant enemy of the Pandavas,

Displaying remarkable valor, Satyaki even succeeded in cutting the wheels of Drona's chariot, crippling the general's mobility and effectiveness. Though he could have killed Drona, Satyaki chose restraint, understanding that victory without honor is no victory at all.

Yet even the bravest fall. Despite his heroics, Satyaki ultimately succumbed in battle, his noble sacrifice a poignant reminder that the strongest warriors fight not for personal glory but for dharma—righteous duty.

Guided by Krishna's divine wisdom, Arjuna returned to the battlefield just in time to avert greater disaster. He decimated the Samsaptaka warriors—a fierce group who had sworn a solemn oath to either defeat Arjuna or perish in the attempt, earning them the name "Sworn Warriors." Despite his efforts, the day's end witnessed heavy losses on both sides, including the death of Drupada, a key ally of the Pandavas, and the fall of Susharma, the king of Trigarta, who fought alongside the Kauravas.

Modern Reflections: Forgiveness in Today's Battlefields

The battlefield has shifted—but the war within rages on.

In today's world, the inability to forgive continues to wreak silent yet sweeping devastation. The weapons are no longer arrows and maces, but emails laced with sarcasm, court petitions steeped in old wounds, and silences between siblings that stretch across decades.

Just as Arjun and Duryodhana's unrelenting pride led to the catastrophic war of Kurukshetra, today we witness boardrooms crumbling, partnerships dissolving, families disintegrating—not because of monumental betrayals, but because of an inability to rise above ego.

Imagine a business venture brimming with potential, undone by a single misstep and two partners too proud to forgive. Or an aged parent dying without seeing their estranged child, both having clung to past grievances instead of healing. Political leaders, too, stoke generational animosities for short-term gains, dragging nations into polarization and conflict—failing to see that peace is not the absence of war, but the presence of reconciliation.

Like Satyaki, the loyal soldier who fought valiantly in the Mahabharata, countless employees today give their all to their organizations. Yet, if leadership is blinded by petty rivalries, even the most devoted efforts are reduced to collateral damage. Pride and grudge become the real adversaries—not the competitor outside, but the bitterness within.

Forgiveness in the Face of Terror

In 2001, Arnold Roth lost his 15-year-old daughter, Malki, in a terrorist bombing in Jerusalem. While seeking justice for the perpetrators, Roth has consistently advocated for dignity, peace, and healing—not hatred. His public statements reflect sorrow, but also an extraordinary refusal to be consumed by bitterness, setting an example for global communities wounded by violence.

Forgiveness, then, is not a passive surrender but an active assertion of inner strength.

It takes immense courage to say: *"Yes, I was hurt, but I choose to let go."* It is the courage to prioritize peace over punishment, growth over grievance. Forgiveness doesn't excuse the wrong, nor does it erase memory—it loosens the chain that ties our future to a painful past.

Research today confirms what ancient wisdom already knew: holding on to resentment harms not just our minds but our bodies—raising blood pressure, weakening immunity, clouding joy. Conversely, forgiveness leads to healthier relationships, reduced stress, and spiritual lightness.

The Mahabharata reminds us:

Wars are not lost on battlefields alone—they are first lost in hardened hearts.

When vengeance becomes the goal, destruction becomes the destiny.

CHAPTER 35

THE COSMIC MANIFESTATIONS

The Veil of Delusion: Man's Limited Vision

The Mahabharata highlights that a deluded mind, clouded by ego and ignorance, cannot perceive the supreme secrets of existence. Arjun, standing on the battlefield, found himself privileged to witness the universal form of Krishna—an overwhelming revelation of the infinite, imperishable self, expressed as Rudra, Adityas, Ashvins, and Maruts across the moving and unmoving elements of the cosmos. This manifestation is often depicted as awe-inspiring and terrifying, showcasing the divine power of Krishna.

This was not ordinary vision. It was only through the divine grace of Krishna that Arjun was granted the spiritual eyes to behold this limitless, splendid spectacle—faces blazing like countless suns, hands wielding conches, tridents, and lotuses—illuminating the ultimate knowledge and destination of all beings.

Awe and Fear: The True Scale of Reality

Arjuna, despite his unparalleled valor, found himself trembling in fear as he beheld Krishna's Virat Swaroop, the divine universal form. In this vision, heaven, earth, and the three worlds converged into a boundless realm of creation and destruction. The infinite vastness of this form overwhelmed Arjuna. He saw countless faces, arms, and eyes, adorned with celestial ornaments, wielding divine weapons. The universe itself seemed to manifest within Krishna's being. This was not a mere sight but a cosmic revelation, an experience that terrified Arjun to his core.

The spectacle before him was so powerful that it seemed to transcend the boundaries of time, space, and even comprehension. Warriors were being consumed by the flaming mouths of Krishna's form, and Arjun witnessed the destruction of the sons of Dhritarashtra and their allies, who were crushed between the cosmic teeth of this divine entity.

"I see no beginning, no end," Arjun exclaimed, acknowledging that the true nature of the universe was far beyond human understanding—a truth that even the most advanced astronomers and scientists struggle to grasp. The mysteries of dark matter and distant galaxies remain an enigma, despite our technological advancements. Arjun realized that the divine vision granted to him was a glimpse of a reality that transcends all human limitations.

The Overwhelming Vision: A Glimpse of Eternity

The sight that Arjun beheld was not just one of beauty; it was awe-inspiring, fearsome, and overwhelming. The cosmic form within Krishna's being contained the infinite expanse of creation and destruction. Arjuna saw not only the entirety of the universe but also the presence of divine beings, sages, and the elements that make up the fabric of existence.

As Arjun's mind struggled to process the magnitude of what he saw, the terrifying and radiant form of Krishna sent waves of fear through him. The sight was not just a visual experience; it was an emotional and spiritual upheaval. He saw the Kauravas, with their allies, rushing headlong into the jaws of Krishna's form like moths rushing into a fire—helpless and doomed. This vision shattered Arjun's sense of security and left him trembling in uncertainty.

Understanding and Transformation: From Fear to Reverence

As the vision continued to unfold, Arjun's perspective shifted. Initially, he was terrified and confused by the vastness of Krishna's cosmic form, but as he absorbed the essence of what he was witnessing, he began to understand. Krishna was not merely his friend or charioteer; He was the embodiment of the universe itself—an infinite, eternal being who contained all time, space, and creation within Himself.

Krishna revealed the ultimate truth:

"I am Time, the mighty destroyer of worlds. I have already slain your enemies. Rise, Arjun! Fight! Become merely my instrument."

In that moment, the illusion of personal doership shattered. Victory and defeat, pride and despair—all were revealed as mere illusions before the cosmic design. Arjun's role was not to act for personal glory, but to align with dharma and to act without attachment.

Arjun saw the three aspects of time—past, present, and future—within Krishna's form. This encapsulated the eternal cycle of creation, preservation, and destruction, reinforcing the idea that Krishna is beyond the confines of temporal existence

This realization was transformative for Arjun. The fear that had initially gripped him began to give way to reverence and respect. Arjun recognized that his role in the battle was not driven by personal motives but by his duty to uphold dharma (righteousness). This understanding led him to embrace his duty, with the knowledge that the war was not merely a fight for victory but a struggle for the establishment of cosmic order.

Modern Reflections: When Power Outpaces Wisdom

Today, we stand at the pinnacle of scientific achievements. Satellites capture distant galaxies; AI deciphers ancient languages; medicine extends life spans. Yet, despite seeing "the universal form" through the lens of modern discovery, humanity often remains blind—driven by ego, greed, and ignorance rather than awe, humility, and noble intent.

Consider the race for technological supremacy. Nations invest billions into developing weapons capable of mass destruction—proud of their prowess, yet forgetting they are like rivers rushing blindly into a fiery mouth. Or think of the individual, racing for material success, blind to the inner void they refuse to confront, much like warriors unaware of the cosmic jaws awaiting them.

Without noble behavior and inner realization, progress turns monstrous. Like Arjun, mankind is offered glimpses of cosmic grandeur, yet fails to transform vision into wisdom.

The Mahabharata warns us:

Power without behavioral nobility leads to self-destruction. Only those who surrender their ego, who act as instruments of a higher purpose, can navigate the terrifying beauty of existence.

The universe does not revolve around human ambition. It is we who must revolve around its eternal truth.

To truly see, one must first bow.

CHAPTER 36

ABHIMANYU: COURAGE BETRAYED BY COWARDICE

Dronacharya's Desperation: Strategy Over Dharma

On the fourteenth day of the war, Dronacharya was under immense pressure. Duryodhana's constant taunts and demands weighed heavily on him. His goal was no longer upholding righteousness – it was simply to capture Yudhishthira at any cost.

Despite commanding thousands, Drona knew the real obstacle was Arjun. As long as Arjun remained, success was impossible. Driven by strategic obsession rather than noble intent, Drona devised the Chakravyuha – a formidable, multi-layered, almost impenetrable battle formation resembling a spinning wheel or lotus. It was designed to trap and destroy.

It was a masterpiece of warcraft, but its purpose was deeply flawed: not to uphold dharma, but to fulfill a king's ego and ambition.

The Chakravyuha: A Web of Betrayal

The Chakravyuha was built like an inescapable maze, designed to confuse, entrap, and eliminate opponents.

Only Krishna and Arjun knew its complete navigation. Arjun, however, was deliberately lured away by Susharma and the Samsaptakas, ensuring he could not protect the Pandava army. Dronacharya, the Kaurava army's commander, needed to create the Chakravyuha formation without Arjun present, as he was one of the few warriors who knew how to penetrate it. By keeping Arjun busy, Drona could successfully implement the Chakravyuha.

Abhimanyu, young and valiant, volunteered to breach the formation. He knew how to enter, but not how to exit. The elders knew this, yet none offered protection or solutions beyond hollow encouragement.

Jayadratha, the king of Sindhu, used a boon from Lord Shiva to prevent the Pandavas, including Bhima, Yudhishthira, and Satyaki, from following Abhimanyu into the Chakravyuha. He was granted the boon to hold off all Pandavas except Arjun for one day, and he used it effectively on the 13th day of the Kurukshetra War to prevent them from entering the Chakravyuha to help Abhimanyu.

Thus, a teenager was thrown into the lions' den, abandoned, and outnumbered not by bravery, but by deliberate betrayal.

The Death of Abhimanyu: Cowardice Unmasked

Abhimanyu fought heroically, killing many mighty warriors—kings, princes, and generals fell to his unmatched vigor.

But seeing themselves unable to subdue a boy fairly, six great warriors—Drona, Karna, Ashwatthama, Kripacharya, Kritavarma, and Dushasana's son—attacked him simultaneously, a blatant violation of war ethics.

On Drona's command, Karna severed Abhimanyu's bow, while other Kaurava warriors killed his charioteer and shattered his chariot. Unarmed, Abhimanyu fought back with a sword, but Drona broke it; he lifted a chariot wheel, only for Karna to smash it. Undeterred, Abhimanyu seized a mace and fiercely attacked the soldiers of Gandhara. Dushasana's son engaged him in a mace duel. Both warriors fell, but Dushasana's son rose first and, striking the defenseless Abhimanyu on the head, killed him.

They broke his chariot, destroyed his weapons, and crippled his defenses. Even then, Abhimanyu fought on with a mace, until he was ultimately murdered in an act of sheer cowardice.

Abhimanyu's death was a brutal violation of the rules of war. After being trapped and overwhelmed by multiple Kaurava warriors, he was forced off his chariot and left defenseless. Severely weakened, he fought valiantly with broken weapons until Dushasana's son struck him fatally. Attacking a fallen warrior was against the martial code, and even among the Kauravas, there was shame over the dishonorable way Abhimanyu was killed.

Where was the vaunted sense of righteousness, the celebrated dharma? It had drowned in the battlefield's blood-soaked mud, alongside honor, courage, and nobility.

A Shattered Dream: Arjun's Vow

When Arjun heard of Abhimanyu's death, he was devastated.

He realized that he, too, had been ensnared—not by enemies outside, but by the decay of values inside his own camp and among the elders he once revered.

Arjuna's grief transformed into rage, and he vowed to slay Jayadratha before sunset the next day. It was no longer a battle for territory or pride. It had become a battle to salvage whatever little honor remained in a war that had long since lost its way.

The Abhimanyu Paradox: Truth Entrapped in the Chakravyuha of Modern Manipulation

In the Mahabharata, the brutal slaughter of Abhimanyu was not just a tactical war maneuver.It was a grim metaphor for what happens when righteousness enters a web of deceit without support. Today, the chakravyuhas haven't disappeared; they've just changed form.

Corporate Chakravyuhas: Strategy Without Soul

A young employee joins a firm full of passion, unaware that his idealism will be used and then discarded. Promised promotions, overburdened with responsibility, and subtly isolated when they question unethical practices. This modern-day Abhimanyu finds himself entrapped in an invisible formation of office politics and power hierarchies.

Performance reviews are weaponized. Loyalty is exploited. Whistleblowers are cornered, not with arrows, but with character assassination, and professional exile.

Political Snares: When Movements Sacrifice Their Soldiers

Grassroots workers rally for a cause, risking safety and reputation. But when the movement gains momentum, they are sidelined to make way for "suitable faces" or convenient alliances. The very hands that built the cause are shackled by betrayal.

These political chakravyuhas mirror the ancient one that ensnared Abhimanyu—multiple layers of strategy cloaked in rhetoric and ambition, all aimed at cornering the inconvenient voice.

Media Manipulation: The Digital Chakravyuha

Today's Dronacharyas and Karnas don't wield celestial weapons—they control narratives. Algorithms silence independent thought. Manipulated hashtags drown dissent. A single truth-teller is encircled by a barrage of misinformation, ridicule, and doctored public opinion.

Abhimanyu didn't die for lack of bravery. He died because others broke the rules to ensure his destruction. So too, truth today is not defeated by lack of merit—but by the systematic violation of integrity by those in power.

Shakuni's Heirs: The Rise of Tactical Manipulation

Shakuni's character from the Mahābhārata is not just a figure of cunning—it is a blueprint of emotional exploitation, psychological manipulation, and strategic sabotage. In modern times, we see this legacy in corporate boardrooms, geopolitical corridors, and social media manipulation.

False promises, carefully planted narratives, and exploitative systems—all bear the fingerprint of Shakuni's ideology. But the Mahābhārata also reminds us: his manipulations led to temporary wins, but eventual ruin.

Countering the Chakravyuha: Lessons from Krishna

In the *Udyoga Parva*, Krishna warns against blind trust and urges discernment. In our era, this means:

- **Emotional regulation**: To not let praise or fear cloud judgment.
- **Critical thinking**: To question intent behind words and acts.
- **Digital vigilance**: To guard against cyber-deceit and psychological targeting.
- **Ethical clarity**: To stand by values, even when manipulation masquerades as progress.

The story of Abhimanyu is not merely a tragedy. It is a recurring question to every generation: will you watch the lone warrior fall, or will you break the Chakravyuha?

Because modern manipulation may be subtle, but its consequences are brutal.

The real challenge of our times is not whether we can identify the Abhimanyus but whether we are willing to become Arjuns who learn from the past, or Krishnas who call out the trap before it's too late.

Will you walk away, or will you enter the formation with your eyes wide open—this time, to break it from within?

History forgets those who won by deceit but immortalizes those who fell with honor.

CHAPTER 37

THE KNOWLEDGE FROM THE WOMB: A LESSON HALF-LEARNT

Ancient Wisdom Before Birth

Stories from various traditions speak of rare souls who remember past lives upon rebirth. However, even rarer are the accounts of knowledge being imparted to a child while still in the mother's womb. In the Mahabharata, a significant example is narrated. The secret of the Chakravyuh was being taught to Subhadra by her husband, Arjuna, while she was pregnant with Abhimanyu. Abhimanyu heard the instruction from within the womb. As the story goes, Subhadra fell asleep midway, and Abhimanyu, from the womb, absorbed only the first part—how to enter the formation but not how to exit it.

This incomplete knowledge sealed Abhimanyu's fate years later on the battlefield, where he could brilliantly breach the Chakravyuha but found himself trapped inside, leading to his tragic and unjust death.

The Injustice That Followed

Abhimanyu's death was not just the result of incomplete training; it exposed the deep cracks in the moral framework of the war. The Kauravas broke the codes of honorable combat by attacking a lone, defenseless, and chariotless warrior in a group. Even respected figures among the Kauravas were ashamed at the way Abhimanyu was killed. His death reflected the erosion of behavioral values and noble intent—the central tragedy that underpins much of the Mahabharata.

Womb Learning: A Forgotten Dialogue

Modern science, especially in the fields of prenatal psychology and gynecology, now re-examines the idea that unborn children absorb emotions, rhythms, and sounds from their mothers. However, the intimate communication once imagined between mother and child seems lost today. In ancient times, this bond was sacred and uninterrupted; now, the hurried lifestyle, social changes, and dual economic burdens have shifted the mother's focus. The womb, once a sanctuary of conscious nurturing, is often drowned out by external noise and stress.

Just as Abhimanyu's incomplete learning led to fatal consequences, modern society too often produces individuals only half-prepared for life's battles—armed with technical skills but deprived of emotional and ethical grounding.

Half Knowledge, Full Consequences: A Modern Reflection

"**A little learning is a dangerous thing;**

Drink deep, or taste not the Pierian spring:"

– *Alexander Pope, An Essay on Criticism*

Abhimanyu's tragedy from the Mahabharata is often retold as a tale of bravery—but at its core lies a chilling caution: the perils of half-knowledge. He knew how to enter the chakravyuha, the most complex war formation, but not how to exit. The consequence? He was trapped, overpowered, and killed.

Now, fast-forward to our world.

Today's Abhimanyus are not on battlefields, but on stages, screens, boardrooms, and timelines. They are the young entrepreneur who reads a few success stories and thinks they're ready to disrupt an industry. They're the teenager who learns how to go viral but not how to handle the fallout of internet fame. They're the student who tops competitive exams but breaks under real-life pressure because they were never taught how to fail gracefully.

In each case, the problem is not the lack of intelligence—it's the illusion of sufficiency.

Pope's quote, "A little learning is a dangerous thing; drink deep, or taste not the Pierian spring," speaks directly to this. The *Pierian spring*, in Greek mythology, was said to give inspiration and knowledge to those who drank from it. But Pope warns: if you sip only a little, you become intoxicated—arrogant, misled, overconfident. Only by drinking deeply, immersing yourself thoroughly in understanding can you achieve true wisdom and humility.

And that's where modern society often falters. We equip people with just enough tools to begin the journey—but not enough to complete it wisely.

We train students to crack entrance exams but not to build resilience.

We teach public speaking but skip listening.

We build apps without understanding ethics.

We shout opinions without context.

We glorify starting—but ignore sustaining and finishing.

Imagine teaching someone how to board a ship in turbulent waters but not how to navigate or dock safely. Wouldn't that be setting them up for disaster? That's what half-knowledge does. It launches us into complexity with no map, no compass, and no lifeboat. Take, for instance, the rise of social media influencers. Many teenagers are taught how to gain followers and create viral content, but rarely are they mentored on how to handle online criticism, misinformation, or the emotional toll of digital overexposure. They know how to enter the world of visibility, but not how to survive in it with dignity.

We open doors without equipping them to walk the entire hallway.

Similarly, imparting knowledge without its ethical completion—knowing how to enter but not how to exit is a dangerous half-truth we continue to pass on.

The danger, as Pope suggests, is that *partial knowledge creates more confidence than competence*. And confidence without competence can be catastrophic.

So the lesson is clear: Don't stop at the gates of knowledge. Don't be content with surface-level learning. Drink deep. Ask more. Understand better. Or else, like Abhimanyu, we might find ourselves applauded at the start, but abandoned at the end—caught in battles we were never fully prepared to fight.

In a world obsessed with entrances, it is the exits we fail to teach—and in that forgotten lesson, noble intent dies.

CHAPTER 38

THE BODY THAT ACTS, THE SOUL THAT WATCHES

The Cosmic Duo: Matter and Spirit

On the battlefield of Kurukshetra, Arjun was not just taught how to fight; he was taught how to *see*. In one of the most layered philosophical moments of the *Bhagavad Gita,* Lord Krishna explains to him the profound relationship between **Prakriti** (the acting body/nature) and **Purusha** (the witnessing soul/consciousness).

Prakriti is the material world—everything we can see, touch, think, feel, or even imagine. It is the body, the senses, the mind, and all their changing states: joy, sorrow, fear, ego, intellect, desire, and aversion.

Purusha, on the other hand, is the silent observer—the *unchanging self* that watches all actions without acting. It is the eternal consciousness that remains untouched even as the world moves and transforms.

Krishna explains:

"Know that the body is the *field,* and he who knows this field is called the *knower* of the field." (*Gita 13.2*)

"The Supreme Soul is said to be beginningless, transcendental, and beyond the three modes of nature, yet it pervades and supports all." (*Gita 13.31*)

Krishna's Simplified Analogy

When Arjun struggles to grasp the abstraction, Krishna offers a metaphor:

- **The body is like a field**—you can sow seeds of karma, but it's always changing, growing, withering.
- **The soul is like the sky**—vast, untouched by weather or dust, witnessing all, yet never entangled.

He says:

"As the sun alone illuminates the entire universe, so does the knower of the field illuminate the whole body by consciousness." (*Gita 13.33*)

The Purusha watches the play of life but remains unmoved. The Prakriti plays endlessly but is powered by the light of the Purusha.

The Misalignment in Mahabharata: Knowledge Without Wisdom

This teaching might seem abstract, but it underscores a crucial flaw in the Mahabharata—**the fundamental disconnect between knowing and being.**

Many warriors—Bhishma, Drona, Karna—had great knowledge (*gyan*) but lacked spiritual alignment (*vivek*). They were *informed*, but not *transformed.*

They acted as **Prakriti unanchored from Purusha**—moved by desire, loyalty, rage, and ego, unaware of the higher consciousness within.

They failed to pause and *watch* before *acting*.

The tragedy? They mistook the battlefield for the entire reality, forgetting the stillness behind the action.

The Science Behind the Metaphor

Interestingly, modern science supports Krishna's insight through a different lens in its own framework.

- **Neuroscience** has begun to distinguish between the "experiencing self" (moment-to-moment thoughts/emotions—akin to *Prakriti*) and the "observing self" (the constant awareness that notices these changes—akin to *Purusha*).

- **Quantum physics** acknowledges that the observer affects the observed—consciousness plays a role in shaping reality, much like Purusha animates Prakriti.

  In both ancient Indian philosophy and modern quantum physics, there's a compelling parallel that suggests consciousness plays a vital role in shaping reality. In *Samkhya* philosophy, Purusha represents pure, unchanging consciousness—the silent witness—while Prakriti is the dynamic, ever-changing material world. Though Purusha does not act, its mere presence is said to animate Prakriti, initiating creation and change. Similarly, in quantum physics, the observer effect shows that a quantum system exists in multiple states until observed—only then does it collapse into a definite reality. This act of observation alters outcomes, mirroring how Purusha's awareness seemingly activates Prakriti. These two frameworks—separated by millennia—suggest a shared insight: consciousness may not be a passive observer but a fundamental force that gives form to matter.

A Modern Reflection: When the Doer Forgets the Watcher

Seeing Without Acting, Acting Without Seeing

A corporate CEO may build an empire, win accolades, and dominate markets—but if they never pause to ask why or at what cost, they are a mere actor lost in the field, blind to the witness within.

A parent may run from school pickups to meetings, all in the name of love—but without awareness, the soul becomes drowned in routine.

A surgeon may save lives with skilled hands, but if he operates without presence, empathy fades into precision, and healing becomes a mechanical task.

An activist may fight for justice with relentless passion, but if rage replaces reflection, they risk becoming what they stand against—reactive, not responsive.

Social media influencers—they perform constantly, reacting to trends, followers, algorithms. They may appear powerful, but are often the most watched and least watching. Their inner self is buried under the pressure of performance.

In all these cases, **Prakriti acts**, but **Purusha sleeps**.

A powerful life is not one that acts the most, but one that watches the clearest before acting. The soul is not here to perform; it is here to witness wisely.

The Final Line: What They Forgot, We Must Remember

In the Mahabharata, the warriors mastered their bodies, honed their intellects, and wielded weapons with godlike precision.

But they never stopped to ask — **who is it that watches? Who is it that acts?**

When we forget the soul that watches, the body that acts becomes a weapon without a purpose.

CHAPTER 39

WRAPPED IN RAGE, BLINDED TO DHARMA

The Night That Broke the Rules

The Mahabharata's thirteenth day of war stands as a chilling testament to what happens when retribution replaces restraint. Traditionally, battles were fought from sunrise to sunset. But on this day, the code of conduct was abandoned. The Chakravyuha formation—an intricate and deadly trap—was designed by the Kauravas to entrap and isolate the young warrior Abhimanyu. Deprived of support, surrounded from all sides, and brutally slaughtered, Abhimanyu became a sacrifice not just to strategy but to collective cruelty.

This savage act triggered Arjun's fury. Blazing with grief, he vowed to kill Jayadrath before sunset the next day. In his single-minded pursuit of vengeance, Arjun cut through seven Akshauhinis of soldiers—nearly 10 million warriors—unleashing divine weapons and laying waste to human lives like they were mere obstacles in his path. In ancient Indian military terminology, an akshauhini is a large military formation, roughly equivalent to a division. It consists of a specific number of chariots, elephants, horses, and foot soldiers.

As the fierce battle raged on, Lord Krishna reminded Arjun of a crucial detail: Jayadratha had received a boon from Lord Shiva that anyone who caused his head to fall to the ground would die instantly. At the same time, Arjun had taken a solemn vow to kill Jayadratha before sunset to avenge the brutal death of his son, Abhimanyu. To fulfill this vow while avoiding the fatal consequence of Shiva's curse, Krishna advised Arjun to behead Jayadratha in such a way that his severed head would not fall to the ground. Arjun used the powerful Indrastra, aiming it so precisely that Jayadratha's head soared through the sky and landed in the lap of his meditating father. Startled by the sudden weight, the father instinctively looked up, causing the head to fall to the ground. The curse was triggered instantly—his skull split in seven places, and he died on the spot.

It was a perfect execution—strategic, precise, and effective. And yet, it was soaked in personal rage.

A War Within a War

The Mahabharata was, at its heart, a war for *dharma*—a fight to restore righteousness and justice in a world where both had been trampled. But within that grand purpose, individual battles often took on a different tone—driven not by dharma but by personal grief, vengeance, and emotional turmoil.

Arjun, for instance, did not slay Jayadratha merely as a warrior executing justice; he did so as a heartbroken father avenging his son Abhimanyu's brutal and unfair death. The scale of destruction he unleashed—including the killing of lakhs of soldiers—was not just strategic; it was deeply emotional. His actions, though justified by war, reflected how easily personal agony can momentarily overshadow the collective cause of righteousness.

A similar moral tension unfolded between Bhima and Vikarna. Vikarna was one of the rare Kauravas who had spoken against Draupadi's humiliation in the Kuru court—an act of conscience that should have aligned him with dharma. But when the time came, Bhima was ordered to kill him. He hesitated, torn between battlefield duty and the memory of Vikarna's earlier stand for justice. And yet, in the relentless logic of war, Vikarna was slain—by the very side his voice once supported.

Even in a war for dharma, there were moments when dharma itself stood silent—eclipsed by grief, loyalty, and the irreversible momentum of vengeance.

Modern Echoes: Rage Dressed in Rationale

Blazing with grief, Arjun vowed to kill Jayadratha before sunset or self-immolate. His pain was genuine, his sense of injustice valid—but his vow was not guided by calm purpose. It was driven by personal loss. In that moment, dharma bent to emotion. It was the fury of a father cloaked in the robes of a warrior. And though he fulfilled his vow, the cost was enormous—the unraveling of reason, the narrowing of purpose, and a battlefield soaked in vengeance rather than justice.

Today, that rage finds new avatars.

Take the case of **a whistleblower in a government office**. Instead of following due process, he leaks sensitive documents to the media—not to reform the system, but to disgrace a superior who once publicly insulted him. The leak, though celebrated by some, causes irreparable damage to diplomatic relations and internal security. What began as a pursuit of truth turns into a spectacle of retribution.

Or picture **a young woman who is ghosted after a long relationship**. She posts private conversations and photos online—not for closure, but to publicly shame her ex. The intent is not healing, but humiliation. The act garners attention and sympathy, but it leaves behind a digital battlefield—mental health scars, reputational loss, and legal battles. Like Arjun's vow, her fury feels justified, but its execution harms far more than the target.

Consider **a teacher publicly reprimanded by a principal during a staff meeting**. Hurt and humiliated, he spends months collecting minor student complaints, manipulating them into a formal complaint letter that goes to the education board. His intent is not student welfare—but institutional revenge. The principal is suspended, morale dips, and trust within the school erodes. Justice, again, becomes the collateral damage of concealed fury.

In each of these, grief morphs into a mission, and the moral compass begins to spin. What looks like courage is often resentment wearing a noble mask.

Take the case of Richard Nixon and the Watergate scandal. What began as political insecurity morphed into unlawful surveillance, covert break-ins, and obstruction of justice. On the surface, it looked like a war against subversion. But peel back the layers, and you find something more human: the fear of humiliation, the sting of opposition, the slow burn of vengeance. His actions were cold and calculated, driven by internal fury at opposition and perceived betrayal. His own recordings (the "Nixon tapes") reveal deep-seated anger, bitterness, and mistrust toward the media, opponents, and even his aides. So while not dramatic like Arjun's fiery vow, it was a simmering, vengeful kind of rage—one masked in strategic language.Nixon wasn't shouting across a battlefield, but his decisions were driven by a deep emotional churn—a desire to crush dissent, not protect democracy. He had all the power, like Arjun. But power clouded by ego becomes its own enemy.

In every era, unprocessed anger doesn't vanish—it adapts.

Sometimes it rides a chariot.

Sometimes it rides a motorcade.

Just like Arjun's oath, modern-day acts of revenge often come with unintended consequences: broken systems, damaged relationships, and blurred lines between justice and vendetta.

CHAPTER 40

THE THREE QUALITIES (GUNAS): UNDERSTOOD, NOT EMBODIED

The Doctrine of the Three Gunas

In his discourse to Arjuna, Lord Krishna reveals a profound truth that underpins both cosmic order and human behavior—the doctrine of the three *gunas*: **sattva** (goodness), **rajas** (passion), and **tamas** (ignorance). These elemental forces of nature shape the internal and external realities of all beings, influencing perception, intent, and action. Sattva is associated with clarity, harmony, and selflessness; rajas with desire, restlessness, and attachment; and tamas with inertia, delusion, and moral blindness. Krishna explains that these gunas bind the *atma* (soul) to *samsara* (the cycle of birth and death), and only those who gain knowledge of the gunas and transcend their influence—through unwavering devotion—can move toward liberation. Yet, knowledge alone is not liberation. As the Mahabharata reveals with piercing honesty, even those who understood these cosmic truths—kings, warriors, sages—often failed to embody them. Their actions, driven by ego or grief, ambition or vengeance, betrayed the very wisdom they possessed. The soul's liberation does not lie in intellectual mastery but in spiritual maturity—a lesson tragically lost on many of the epic's most powerful characters. Just as poison cannot be detected by sight but only by its effect, the presence of a guna is revealed through the choices it provokes. And thus, the Mahabharata becomes not just a tale of war, but a mirror held up to human frailty—showing how sacred knowledge without *noble intent* becomes impotent, even dangerous.

The Trap of Self Delusion

One of Krishna's most piercing insights in the Gita is that self-delusion masquerades as righteousness. Every individual, he explains, tends to glorify the *guna* that most dominates them. The person governed by *rajas* sees action, ambition, and control as noble. The one steeped in *tamas* justifies inaction, blame, and denial as pragmatism. Even the *sattvic*—the supposedly enlightened—may silently harbor pride in their goodness, mistaking moral self-satisfaction for true humility. Thus, each person believes themselves just, even when entangled in illusion.

The Mahabharata lays bare this psychological trap with brutal clarity. Arjun, though chosen by Krishna himself and the recipient of divine counsel, is overtaken by blinding sorrow after the brutal slaying of his son Abhimanyu. His grief cloaks itself in dharma, but his revenge is emotionally charged—not spiritually elevated. His *sattvic* grounding is temporarily drowned by *rajasic* rage. Bhima, the embodiment of strength and fierce loyalty, kills Vikarna—a brother who once opposed Draupadi's disrobing. Though his conscience flickers in hesitation, Bhima proceeds, citing duty as his justification. The gunas play out not in abstract theory but in the battlefield of choice, where emotion often wins over wisdom.

Krishna's teaching is unambiguous: mere knowledge is no guarantee of virtue. Knowing the gunas, quoting scriptures, or even being Krishna's confidante does not ensure noble action. The Kurukshetra war is not short of learned men—Bhishma, Drona, Kripacharya—all deeply versed in dharma. Yet restraint, self-awareness, and moral clarity are rare. The tragedy is not ignorance, but the failure to *embody* what one already knows.

In modern terms, it's the CEO who preaches ethics but exploits labor, the teacher who speaks of empathy but belittles struggling students, or the activist who champions peace but rages with personal vendetta. Like poisoned water in a golden goblet, knowledge without behavior is deceptive—and dangerous.

In the end, the greatest battle is not fought on the field, but within: between what we know and what we choose to do.

Beyond the Binding Threads: True Liberation from the Gunas

Krishna reveals a path rarely walked—the transcendence of the three *gunas*. The truly liberated soul, He says, is not merely *sattvic, rajasic,* or *tamasic,* but free from the sway of all three. This elevated being remains untouched by the dualities of life—praise and blame, success and failure, joy and grief. Such a person treats gold and clay with the same regard, shows equal composure before friend or enemy, and performs actions not out of craving or fear, but from a place of deep stillness. This is the *sthitaprgna*—one established in unwavering wisdom.

But in the epic landscape of the Mahabharata, how many rose to this rare state? The contrast between knowledge and embodiment is striking. Bhishma, the guardian of dharma, was revered for his intellect and restraint. Yet he remained bound by his vow and loyalty to the throne, even when the throne was unjust. Drona, a master of scriptures and warfare, chose allegiance to Hastinapura over conscience, despite knowing the moral emptiness of the Kaurava cause. These were men of profound wisdom—but wisdom that did not liberate them. Their actions were still entangled in *rajasic* obligation and *tamasic* fear of dishonor.

Krishna's message is subtle but powerful: liberation is not about knowing the gunas—it is about no longer being ruled by them. It is the internal freedom to choose conscience over compulsion, clarity over confusion. While many in the Mahabharata could recite dharma, few could live it when it cost them everything.

In transcending the gunas, one does not renounce life—but its compulsions. Only then does action become free, and the soul, unbound.

The Modern Mirror: Knowledge Without Conduct is Not Wisdom

In today's world, moral superiority often wears a polished suit. Picture a corporate leader who quotes ancient scriptures, hosts seminars on ethical leadership, and promotes a culture of "values." Yet, when a younger colleague begins to shine, or a project threatens to expose flaws, the same leader may quietly stall promotions, reassign credit, or subtly undermine dissent—all while maintaining the façade of integrity.

This isn't a lack of knowledge. It's a dominance of *rajas*—the guna of ambition and insecurity—parading as righteousness. Like many warriors in the Mahabharata who understood dharma but faltered in action, modern figures, too, fall into the gap between knowing and being.

The same pattern plays out across industries. Consider the industrialist who donates generously to charity but refuses to implement basic labour welfare measures in their own factories—fair wages, safe conditions, healthcare. Or the academician who teaches social justice but belittles colleagues, fearing the dilution of their intellectual spotlight. These are not failures of intellect but of embodiment—where the ego cleverly co-opts virtue for self-preservation.

True transcendence, as Krishna insists, is not about how much one knows, but how one chooses to act when comfort, authority, or prestige is at stake. It is when a business owner chooses long-term ethical practice over short-term profit, when a manager protects a whistleblower instead of silencing them, when a teacher uplifts rather than competes with their students.

In every sphere—corporate, academic, political—the test of one's *guna* lies not in public image but in private decisions. To know is easy. To live it when no one is watching—that is liberation.

The tragedy of the Mahabharata lies not in ignorance, but in the failure to act on wisdom. Nearly every key figure knew the path of dharma. What was missing was the behavioral integrity to walk it.

Wisdom begins not with knowing the gunas, but with seeing how they move within us—quietly shaping what we justify, excuse, and glorify

CHAPTER 41

THE PRICE OF A HALF-TRUTH

The Banyan Tree and the Search for Truth

In the Bhagavad Gita, Krishna describes to Arjun a sacred and symbolic tree—the Ashvattha, or the upside-down banyan tree. Its roots reach upward into the spiritual realm, while its branches spread downward into the material world. Its leaves, said to be the hymns of the Vedas, represent divine wisdom. Krishna presents this inverted tree as a metaphor for human existence: rooted in the eternal, yet entangled in illusion. The branches symbolize desires, attachments, and the cycle of birth and death, while the roots call us back to our divine source. The tree appears real, but like a reflection in water, it is an illusion—misleading and deceptive unless understood with spiritual clarity. This imagery mirrors the essence of the Mahabharata, where truth itself is tested and twisted. Yudhishthir, revered for his honesty, speaks a half-truth that blurs moral boundaries. Karna, torn between loyalty to his friend and the blood that binds him to his brothers, stands suspended in a tragic dilemma. Just as the branches of the Ashvattha can both shelter and ensnare, the characters in the epic must navigate the illusions of dharma, identity, and choice. The journey to truth, like the path to liberation, begins with recognizing the illusion—and daring to see beyond it.

The Slow Unraveling of Dharma

As the war dragged into its fifteenth day, the landscape of Kurukshetra bore more than blood—it bore exhaustion, quiet treachery, and desperation to win at any cost. The Pandavas, once paragons of righteousness, now leaned into strategies that blurred the lines between duty and deceit.

The turning point came with Dronacharya—commander of the Kaurava forces and teacher to both sides. After slaying Drupada and Virata, Drona remained nearly invincible, empowered by celestial weapons and resolve. But Krishna, ever the strategist, saw a chink in his armor—not in his skills, but in his heart: his love for his son, Ashwatthama.

Yudhishthira's Whisper: The Fine Print of Righteousness

A calculated plan was devised to dismantle one of the most formidable warriors on the battlefield—Dronacharya. Knowing that Drona's emotional anchor was his son, the Pandavas sought to strike not with arrows, but with grief. Bhima killed an elephant named Ashwatthama—who happened to share its name with Drona's son—and loudly proclaimed, "Ashwatthama is dead!"

Confused and shaken, Drona turned to Yudhishthira, the man famed for never telling a lie. Pressured by strategy and dharma twisted by desperation, Yudhishthira muttered, "Ashwatthama is dead," and then softly added, almost inaudibly, "the elephant."

According to legend, Yudhishthira's chariot used to float slightly above the ground because of his unwavering commitment to truth. But the moment he spoke that half-truth about Ashwatthama, the chariot's wheels touched the earth—signifying a fall in his moral stature.

This small breach in truth shattered Drona's inner resolve. Stricken by what he believed was the death of his only son, he lost the will to fight. In stunned silence, he laid down his arms and closed his eyes, withdrawing inward. It was then that Dhrishtadyumna—the son of Drupada, who had vowed to avenge his father's death at Drona's hands—stepped forward and beheaded the defenceless master. This was not the code of Kshatriyas. It wasn't battle. It was cold, calculated execution under the guise of war.

With Drona's fall, the command of the Kaurava army passed to Karna, shifting the war into a new, bloodier phase—one still shadowed by moral disintegration.

A Mother's Appeal, A Warrior's Promise

Away from the roar of the battlefield, a quieter but no less significant encounter unfolded—between Kunti and her firstborn, Karna. In a secret meeting, Kunti revealed what Karna already knew from Krishna: that he was her son, the eldest of the Pandavas, born before her marriage and abandoned out of fear and shame.

With trembling words, Kunti did not plead for loyalty, nor did she ask him to betray Duryodhana, the one man who had accepted him without hesitation.

Instead, she made a mother's request: to spare his brothers—the Pandavas—if fate allowed.

Karna was torn between blood and bond—a biological son of Kunti, yet raised by a charioteer's family and fiercely loyal to Duryodhana. He was torn between duty and blood. He promised her this much: he would fight Arjuna to the death, but the others he would not harm. Her five sons would remain five—either Arjuna or he would fall, but never both.

This was a rare act of restraint in a war that had devoured kin and shattered bonds. Amidst the storm of revenge, Karna's vow was a final gesture to preserve at least one strand of love in a world unraveling.

When Compassion Defies the Chaos

Drona's death marked more than the end of a military strategist—it signaled the downfall of a moral order. A revered teacher was not brought down in fair combat, but through a cruel twist of emotion. His love for his son was exploited, his clarity clouded by manipulated grief. He was not vanquished by steel, but by sorrow—cheated by those who once revered him.

In contrast, Karna's pact with Kunti was not just a tender moment between a mother and her long-lost son—it was an agonizing moral crossroads. He stood torn between two worlds: loyalty to Duryodhana, the only man who gave him dignity when society turned its back and the newly acknowledged bond with the mother who had abandoned him. Choosing not to kill his brothers was not weakness. It was strength of a different kind—the kind that defies vengeance in favor of love, even in a war built on revenge.

In a battlefield ruled by might and strategy, Karna's restraint—and Drona's collapse—remind us that the deepest battles are not fought with weapons, but within the human heart.

Modern Parallels: Half-Truths in High Places

In today's world, ethical betrayal rarely arrives with a sword—it comes dressed in semantics. Today, battlefields look different—but the moral dilemmas remain uncannily familiar. We see them not in blood-soaked soil, but in contracts, corridors, and quiet corners of decision-making

- A **hospital** advertises free surgeries for the underprivileged—but patients are charged for "preliminary assessments" and "mandatory consultations," which cost more than the surgery itself.
- A **school** promises "100% scholarships" for the meritorious—but the condition lies in the asterisk: only on tuition, not books, transport, or uniforms.
- A **government official** may uphold constitutional values in public speeches, while manipulating facts to pass unjust laws quietly in emergency sessions.
- A **pharmaceutical company** promotes a "breakthrough drug" with disclaimers buried

so deep that the long-term risks are never fully known until harm is irreversible.

- A **glossy investment brochure** may promise "guaranteed returns," but the real truth—about risks, lock-ins, or hidden fees—lies buried in fine print, whispered like Yudhishthira's "Ashwatthama is dead...the elephant." Legally correct, ethically evasive. The truth exists, but is hidden in size and placement—intentionally overlooked, deliberately quiet. In modern contracts, the most devastating clauses are never shouted—they're buried in fonts too small for human attention. Like Yudhishthira's whisper, they don't lie—but they don't reveal, either
- In **corporate boardrooms**, CEOs preach "employee-first" culture, yet approve mass layoffs via impersonal emails—decisions rooted in strategy, not empathy. The language of compassion is carefully curated for public reports, while reality whispers otherwise.

Like the banyan tree, such systems give shade but demand no accountability for their tangled roots.

These are not failures of awareness—they are failures of alignment. The mind may know what is noble, but the heart and hand often choose what is convenient.

In an age of loud declarations, it is the whispered truths that reveal the real character.

In a war of truths and half-truths, it is not the sword that wounds deepest, but the silence between what is said and what is meant. When power outpaces conscience, and truth is disguised in fine print, the war of Kurukshetra never truly ends—it just shifts from chariots to chairs of influence.

CHAPTER 42

BETWEEN DIVINITY AND DARKNESS: THE CHOICE OF HUMAN CONDUCT

Krishna's Revelation: The Two Paths

In the *Mahabharata,* we already see how good and bad can mix within the same person. Yudhishthir tells a half-truth to win a war. Karna remains loyal to a friend even though it means going against his own brothers. These choices show us a deeper truth—the divine and the demonic both live within us, and which side wins depends on the choices we make.

In the *Bhagavad Gita,* Krishna explains to Arjun that every person—and even every object—has either a divine or demonic nature. This isn't just a symbol or story. It's a way to understand human behavior and the world around us.

Divine nature comes from good qualities: honesty, courage, kindness, self-control, and the desire to help others. People with these traits are calm, clear in thought, and act without selfishness. They give freely, let go of things without sadness, and live with purpose and peace. Their presence uplifts others.

Demonic nature, on the other hand, is not about demons from stories. It's about harmful traits in real life—pride, anger, greed, lies, arrogance, and the constant need for power and pleasure. People with these qualities chase after things endlessly, but never feel satisfied. They think the world has no moral order—that life is just about luck and desire. Even when they give or pray, it's only to show off or get something in return. Deep down, they are restless, anxious, and lost.

The message is simple but powerful: Your nature is shaped by your actions, not by your birth. If you choose truth, compassion, and humility, you grow closer to the divine. If you choose selfishness and pride, you drift toward darkness.

Nature's Clues: Stones That Shine, Rivers That Weep

Krishna says that divine and demonic qualities are not limited to humans. Even nature reflects these qualities—in how stones, plants, and rivers behave and serve others.

In nature, the divine is often found where one least expects it. Consider the polished stones resting quietly in riverbeds—once rough, they have been shaped by suffering: detached from mountains, rolled by currents, scarred by friction. They don't resist, don't complain. It is their endurance through adversity that gives them their sheen. They become sacred, even worshipped, not for their origin, but for their transformation. It doesn't resist, doesn't complain. It becomes round and polished—not by force, but by surrender. It is no longer jagged with ego; its very erosion becomes a metaphor for selfless offering. That smooth stone is no longer sharp or selfish. It becomes beautiful and sacred because it allowed itself to be changed. People even pick up such stones and worship them—not because of where they came from, but because of what they became.

Or take the flowers offered to gods—many grow not in well-tended gardens but in wild, harsh places. Without manure or water, in isolation, they thrive. They do not discriminate between rich or poor—they are free for all. Their quiet, uncompromising existence teaches us that true purity needs no pedestal. Consider plants like tulsi or bilva. They don't grow in rich soil or don't need special care. They grow in dry, lonely places—without attention or help. And yet, they are used in worship. Why? Because they symbolize purity, selflessness, and quiet strength. They don't grow to show off. They grow to serve—available to everyone, asking for nothing in return.

In the past, we saw rivers as sacred. People would bathe in them to cleanse not just the body, but also the mind. We saw river water as pure and healing. Today, those same rivers are polluted and choked with waste. We still need rivers—but we no longer respect them.

We used to pick up smooth river pebbles and see in them a symbol of how pain and patience shape us into something better. Today, we throw them away or walk over them without any thought. We used to gather these pebbles and worship them—seeing in their journey a metaphor for human evolution through trials. Now, they are trampled underfoot or discarded for being "useless."

Even sacred plants that once grew wild and free are now sold in shops. Today, we patent their names, bottle their essence, and sell them in the marketplace of health fads. We bottle their oils, brand their names, and chase trends—forgetting their real value lies in their simplicity and service, not in their market price.

The truth is, nature still holds divine wisdom. But we've stopped looking. We don't suffer from ignorance—we suffer because we don't live by the values we already know..

Krishna's message was never about who you are by birth—it was about how you behave. If we continue to pollute rivers, sell sacred plants, and ignore the quiet beauty of nature, we don't just lose our connection to the environment—we lose our connection to the divine within ourselves.

These insights may seem ancient, but they reverberate urgently in our modern world. We do not suffer for lack of knowledge, but for lack of behavioral integrity. Krishna's distinction between divine and demonic was never about caste or class—it was about conduct.

The Three Gates to Hell

Krishna warns that lust, anger, and greed are the three gateways to hell. If we keep choosing these, we fall deeper into confusion and suffering. They are ever open, ever inviting. We walk through them willingly. Once inside, the soul forgets discernment. Demonic nature is a consequence of repeated rejection of wisdom and duty. It doesn't arise from a single act, but from repeated choices that ignore one's inner sense of right and wrong. It is not the result of one mistake, but of a pattern of misdeeds that slowly erodes moral clarity. We mistake indulgence for success, aggression for strength, and accumulation for fulfillment. And yet, none of these lead to lasting peace.

Modern Reflections: The Polished Resume and the Corroded Soul

Elizabeth Holmes was once seen as a genius entrepreneur. At just 19, she started a company called **Theranos**, which claimed it could test for hundreds of diseases using just a few drops of blood. The idea sounded revolutionary—and many powerful people believed her.

Her company raised over $700 million from big investors, and at its peak, Theranos was valued at $10 billion. Holmes appeared on magazine covers, gave public talks, and was compared to Steve Jobs.

But there was one major problem: the technology didn't actually work.

Instead of being honest and fixing the problem, Holmes chose to lie. She showed fake test results, misled doctors, patients, and investors, and kept promoting the company as a success.

Over time, the truth came out. Holmes and her business partner, Sunny Balwani, were charged with fraud. Both were found guilty and sentenced to prison.

Why this matters:

Elizabeth Holmes had everything—a glowing résumé, public praise, and a powerful image. But behind the scenes, her choices were slowly corroding her integrity.

Like Krishna's warning about the slow rise of the "asuric" (demonic) nature—this wasn't a single dramatic fall. It happened little by little—through excuses, lies, and the belief that success was more important than truth.

Today, the demonic nature doesn't always arrive with weapons or war cries. More often, it slips quietly into daily life—through pride, entitlement, and silent acts of exploitation. Like the executive who rewards himself with massive bonuses while laying off hundreds of employees. Or the student who cheats "just once" to protect a grade. These acts may seem small, but each one reflects what Krishna warned us about: the slow erosion of morality.

It doesn't happen in one moment. The tree of demonic nature grows from repeated choices—watering it with selfishness, feeding it with excuses, and pruning away our inner voice.

Take the social media influencer who fakes charity for likes, while ignoring actual need. Or the professional who steals ideas but cloaks it in smooth presentations. These aren't crimes in the traditional sense—but they chip away at the soul.

We live in a world that celebrates resumes polished like river stones—but we rarely ask: what shaped the person behind them? Was it genuine service or strategic self-promotion? Is the smoothness the result of experience—or a mask worn for applause?

True refinement, like a river stone, comes from enduring friction and learning from it. A boulder becomes sacred not because it is seen, but because it has been shaped—through hardship, humility, and quiet transformation.

Unless we start choosing refinement over reaction, restraint over indulgence, and wisdom over pride, we will remain trapped in between—neither fully fallen nor fully free.

In a world obsessed with appearances, we forget: a boulder becomes sacred not because it is seen, but because it has been shaped—enduring, falling, rising. The divine is not a label; it is a result of refinement.

The divine and the demonic are not distant myths—they are choices we make each day. In what we say, avoid, justify, or pursue. A sacred life isn't one without error, but one shaped by self-awareness, correction, and quiet strength. What polishes the soul is not applause, but alignment with truth—even when no one is watching.

We are not born divine or demonic—

we become what we preserve within and permit around us.

The true Mahabharata is not between enemies,

but between the purity we defend and the poison we justify.

CHAPTER 43

THE SEVENTEENTH DAY: WHEN GLORY FORGETS GRACE

The Fire That Would Not Die

The battlefield of Kurukshetra was never short of warriors—it was short of wisdom. The 17th day of the Mahabharata war stands out not just for the violence it witnessed, but for the stubborn persistence on both sides to win, no matter the cost. It was a day of brilliant strategy and deep symbolism, but also of crumbling restraint.

Karna, commanding the Kaurava army, created the *Surya Vyuha* —a military formation based on the sun, symbolizing light, power, clarity, and vision. Fittingly so, for Karna was born of Surya and believed this vyuha would offer him both physical protection and spiritual clarity. At the heart of the formation was Duryodhana, shielded by Karna and an elite circle of warriors—Shalya, Kripacharya, Shakuni, Kritavarman, and Ashwathama.

On the other side, Arjun led the Pandava forces with *Mahisha Vyuha,* shaped like the horn of a buffalo—known for its brute strength, wild charge, and uncompromising rage. At its center sat Yudhishthira, the dharmic anchor of the Pandavas side.

As the day wore on, Karna unleashed the Bhargavastra, a terrifying weapon that devastated the

Pandava ranks. Arjun, for a moment, admitted he could not counter it. Yet he refused to abandon his soldiers. Instead of reacting with pride or panic, he chose to stand between the weapon and his people, absorbing both fire and responsibility.

The Hidden Exhaustion Behind Glory

As swords clashed and arrows lit up the sky, a deeper weariness began to take hold—not just of the body, but of the spirit. It was not only physical fatigue that crept across the battlefield, but also a moral fatigue—the slow erosion of clarity, restraint, and righteous purpose.

The warriors on both sides displayed remarkable bravery, refusing to retreat despite exhaustion and loss. Yet, valor alone does not make a war just. Beneath the courage, cracks had begun to show.

Karna, burning with the need to prove himself superior to Arjun, was driven less by duty and more by old wounds—rejection, humiliation, and the desperate need for validation. His bow carried not only arrows but the heavy burden of unresolved pain. Karna fought with flawless technique driven by resentment and the need to prove his worth. Though noble in generosity, he lacked clarity in moral direction. He gave his loyalty to Duryodhana, a flawed leader, and thus fought for a cause that betrayed the very virtues he embodied.

Arjun, in contrast, had a clear purpose—fighting to uphold dharma—but briefly wavered. His reluctance wasn't cowardice but a momentary spiritual fatigue, a fog of emotion that dulled his focus. It was Krishna who reminded him that this battle was not personal revenge, but a duty to truth. Once realigned, Arjun fought with terrifying precision and ended Karna's journey

They pushed him to rise above emotion, to align strength with purpose. Once awakened, Arjun unleashed a renewed force—clear, fierce, and focused. His transformation shifted the balance of power that changed the tide—and sealed Karna's fate.

Day Seventeen: A Turning Point Etched in History

The 17th day of the Mahabharata war was more than a clash of strategies—it was the emotional and moral climax of the conflict, where two of its finest warriors, Karna and Arjun, stood at personal crossroads.

Historically, the 17th has often signaled moments of dramatic transition—moments of political liberation, moral reckoning, and national transformation. September 17, for instance, marks Hyderabad's liberation—a shift from princely rule to democratic integration. In the Mahabharata, too, the 17th day marked the fall of Karna, a hero known for his boundless charity but tragic allegiance.

He died with dignity, his loyalty unshaken—but his path, misdirected. The lesson is stark: even the noblest virtues lose meaning when they serve the wrong cause.

True greatness lies not just in how fiercely we fight but in why we fight.

Modern Echoes: When Brilliance Outruns Conscience

Not all battles today are fought for land or legacy—many are waged quietly, in the grey zones of influence, innovation, and ambition. The 17th day of the war was a turning point not because of brute force, but because it exposed a misalignment of moral clarity and strategic skill.

In today's Kurukshetras the weapons have changed—algorithms, media influence, economic leverage—but the battle between conscience and competence rages on.

We continue to reward precision and performance, yet rarely pause to examine the intent behind action. The world applauds results, but forgets to ask what was sacrificed to achieve them.

Imagine a tech innovator who builds a revolutionary social media platform or a mobile gaming app. It's sleek, intuitive, and addictive—and within a year, it has billions of users worldwide. The app skyrockets in valuation, the founder is hailed as a genius, invited to speak at global summits, and earns titles like "Disruptor of the Year."

But beneath the success story is a darker truth:

- Teenage mental health plummets, as young users get hooked on endless scrolling, likes, and digital validation.

- Sleep disorders rise, especially among children and adolescents, due to late-night use.
- Anxiety, comparison, and loneliness become silent epidemics—even as engagement metrics soar.
- Meanwhile, the app's algorithm is intentionally designed to maximize screen time, attention capture, and emotional response—because more time equals more profit.

This is a real-world 'vyuha': a dazzling creation but no ethical spine.

The innovator is not evil, just like Karna was not evil. He may even claim he just built what people wanted. But by refusing to take responsibility for the impact, he becomes a part of the problem.

This mirrors Karna's journey on the 17th day. His skills were unmatched, his loyalty unshakeable but his alignment was flawed. Similarly, today's innovators can become unwitting agents of harm when they allow brilliance to outrun behavioral responsibility.

A sharp mind can change the world—but without conscience, it can just as easily damage it.

In a world obsessed with metrics, likes, patents, and influence, clarity of purpose has become the first casualty. The vyuhas today are intellectual, digital, economic—but the question remains unchanged: Do we still know why we fight, build, or lead?

The 17th day reminds us: impact without alignment isn't power—it's peril in disguise.

In our world, victory without virtue is just another kind of defeat—dressed well, applauded loudly, but empty at its core.

When brilliance outruns conscience, progress becomes peril.

CHAPTER 44

ACTING WITH PURPOSE: WHY RIGHT ACTION NEEDS RIGHT INTENT

Purity of Action: Beyond the Surface

As the war raged around him, Arjun turned inward with a question that was not about weapons, strategy, or winning. He asked Krishna: *How should one live meaningfully?* Should worship be guided by personal beliefs or scriptural wisdom? Behind this question lay a profound moral confusion.

Krishna pointed out that even noble-looking acts—like charity, sacrifice, or fasting—can be deeply flawed if driven by ego, pride, or greed.

- Fasting to impress others
- Charity and donations to earn praise
- Speaking 'truth' laced with cruelty—

These are not acts of virtue but of self-glorification. True austerity, Krishna taught, lies in discipline without expectation, speech that uplifts, and charity that respects time, place, and worthiness.

Even something as simple as the food we consume reflects our alignment.

- Fresh, wholesome food nurtures clarity and goodness.

- Overindulgent, spicy, or stale food clouds the mind and body.

Every choice, no matter how small, builds or breaks character.

The Language of Faith: Om Tat Sat

Krishna offered Arjun a final compass—three syllables to guide all human endeavor: **Om**, **Tat**, and **Sat**.

- **Om** signifies a sacred beginning—anchoring any action in divine consciousness.
- **Tat** removes personal ego—detaching the act from selfish motives or reward.
- **Sat** affirms truth—ensuring that the act serves a higher, enduring purpose.

These aren't just ritualistic sounds. They represent the spirit in which action must be performed. Sacrifice, penance, and charity—no matter how elaborate—mean nothing when done with pride, greed, or mindless tradition.

When faith is absent, the act is Asat—false. It brings no true fruit, in this life or the next.

Krishna explained that even good actions—like eating the right food, following discipline, or giving to others—can become harmful if done with the wrong intention.Austerity that harms the body out of ego, or charity given for social display, may look noble—but they are inwardly hollow with no real spiritual value inside.

Modern Parallels: The Mask of Morality

Krishna's discourse is not a rejection of rituals, charity, or discipline—but a warning: when the *why* is rotten, the *what* loses meaning. This warning resonates now more than ever.

Consider these modern echoes:

- **The Corporate CSR Trap**
- A multinational company donates crores to climate causes, plants trees in barren zones, and advertises its "green heart." Behind the scenes, it lobbies for deregulating emission standards and dumps toxic waste in rural rivers.
- *Charity without conscience becomes corporate camouflage.*
- **Performative Activism**
- A celebrity "fasts" for a social cause, goes live on Instagram, and gains millions of views. But his products are made in sweatshops, and they do nothing when real change is needed.
- *This is austerity done for applause – Rajasic in form, Tamasic in effect.*
- **The Diet Culture Obsession**
- Influencers glamorize extreme detoxes, juice cleanses, and 3-hour workouts—not as a spiritual discipline. Their followers silently develop eating disorders and body shame.

- *Discipline divorced from wisdom becomes self-harm in disguise.*
- **Misguided Philanthropy**
- A tech mogul donates to build temples and schools but refuses to pay fair wages to his staff or ensure safe working conditions in his warehouses.
- *Tamasic charity—given at the wrong time, to the wrong recipients, for the wrong reason.*

Krishna's message is timeless:

What you do is not enough. Why you do it, how you do it, and with what inner posture—these define the true measure of your morality.

In a world where virtue is often rehearsed but rarely lived, clarity of intention is the rarest form of intelligence.

These are the modern rituals—slick, well-packaged, and applauded. But like sacrifices performed without faith, they leave no lasting value. They are today's *Asat*—truthless actions veiled in glamour.

CHAPTER 45

THE FINAL BLOW: WHEN RULES CRUMBLED AND INTENT WAS EXPOSED

The Eighteenth Day: A War Without Honour

The death of Karna on the seventeenth day of the Mahabharata war left the Kaurava army shattered. In desperation, Shalya was appointed the next commander-in-chief. The war, now stripped of strategy and grace, turned into a brutal scramble for survival.

That very night—without waiting for sunrise—the few surviving warriors from the Kaurava side, including Ashwatthama, Kripacharya, Kritavarma, and the injured Duryodhan, launched a surprise attack on the sleeping Pandava camp.What followed was not war, but a massacre. Ashwatthama entered the camp and slaughtered five sleeping sons of Draupadi, mistaking them for the Pandavas. Unarmed soldiers were murdered in their sleep. There was no battlefield, no warning, and no honour.

Ashwatthama, driven by revenge, unleashed the Brahmāstra—a powerful divine weapon—against the pregnant Uttara, Abhimanyu's wife, in a desperate attempt to destroy the Pandava lineage. However, Krishna intervened and saved the unborn child, Parikshit. Though Krishna had tolerated many breaches of dharma during the war in pursuit of a greater good, he could not justify this act. He condemned Ashwatthama's massacre and his attack on Uttara as deeply sinful and unjust. As punishment, Krishna cursed him to wander the earth for eternity, afflicted by disease and isolation. Ashwathama's fate serves as a powerful lesson in the Mahabharat about the consequences of one's actions and the importance of dharma (righteousness). His story is a poignant reminder of the enduring impact of vengeance and violence.

Duryodhan's Defeat: A Fall From Honour

The war did not end with Ashwatthama's massacre. Duryodhan, terrified and humiliated, fled the battlefield and hid in a lake to avoid death. When Balarama returned from his pilgrimage and found him, he urged Duryodhan to face his fate and not act like a coward. Eventually, Duryodhan agreed to fight Bhima in a mace duel—one final attempt to salvage his pride and uphold a warrior's dignity.

But even this last battle broke the code of honour. Bhima, remembering his vow after Draupadi's humiliation during the dice game, was determined to exact revenge. Bhima, advised by Krishna, strategically struck Duryodhana on the thighs —an area forbidden in mace combat. This was an act considered dishonorable in warfare and was debated for its fairness. The blow shattered Duryodhan's body and spirit. Though he died a warrior's death, it came not with dignity, but in dishonour.

Duryodhan's end symbolized the moral collapse on both sides of the war. The Kurukshetra battle closed not with a righteous victory, but with a battlefield stained by broken vows and abandoned ethics.

Numbers and Symbolism: The Significance of Eighteen

The number 18 holds deep symbolic meaning across the Mahabharata and Hindu scriptures. It is more than a number—it marks pivotal moments and structured cycles in sacred texts:

- The Mahabharata itself is divided into 18 parvas (sections).
- The Bhagavad Gita, a spiritual guide within the epic, has 18 chapters.
- The Kurukshetra war raged for 18 days.
- A total of 18 army divisions participated in the war—11 from the Kauravas and 7 from the Pandavas.

This repetition is not incidental. In Hindu tradition, the number 18 often symbolizes the completion of a cycle, a decisive culmination of an intense struggle—whether it's the war between good and evil, or the inner conflict between one's higher and lower self.

There are 18 Puranas, 18 Upa-puranas, and 18 Dharma Shastras as well, reinforcing its association with spiritual and moral frameworks. It represents the point of reckoning where choices crystallize into outcomes.

But the final, eighteenth day of the war delivers a bitter truth. It doesn't glorify victory—it reveals the moral fatigue and ethical compromises on both sides. Ashwatthama's night massacre, Bhima's unlawful strike, and Duryodhan's dishonourable death all expose the erosion of values in the pursuit of winning.

Thus, in the Mahabharata, 18 becomes not just a number of triumph—but a mirror to reflect on what is lost in the name of victory.

Modern Reflection: The Bodyline Series - When Cricket Lost Its Gentleman's Code

In the early 1930s, Australia's Don Bradman was nearly unstoppable in cricket. His batting average was phenomenal, and England feared losing the Ashes again. To counter him, the English team (under captain Douglas Jardine) developed a tactic called "Bodyline"—fast bowlers would aim at the batsman's body, with fielders placed close to catch deflections. Though not *illegal,* it was against the spirit of the game.

The tactic injured players, sparked public outrage, and nearly caused a diplomatic rift between England and Australia. Though England won the series, they were heavily criticized.

Why this is relevant

- England followed the letter of the rules but broke the spirit—just like in the Mahabharata, where many actions (like killing Karna when he was unarmed) were technically "within rules," but morally questionable.

- The intent—to dominate at any cost—stood exposed.
- The victory felt tarnished, and it raised deeper questions:
- *"If you have to break honour to win, is that win worth remembering?"*
- The battlefield isn't always war—it can be a cricket pitch
- Just like in Kurukshetra, the deeper wound wasn't physical but ethical. And once intention becomes suspect, even the fairest-looking act begins to rot from within.

When History Whispers Warnings: A Modern-Day Mirror

Duryodhan's end is not just a tale of personal defeat—it is a warning. In modern times, we see echoes of this story in leaders who cling to power even when their cause has collapsed Like Duryodhan hiding in a lake, some disappear into curated narratives, PR makeovers, or selective truths, avoiding accountability until they are forced into the open. They hope time will bury the consequences of their actions. But evading responsibility often invites a more humiliating downfall. Duryodhan's end is more than a historical moment—it is a powerful allegory for what happens when pride clouds judgment and rules are bent to suit personal agendas. Truth has a way of resurfacing, and the delay only deepens disgrace.

Bhima's final illegal blow—delivered under Krishna's counsel—forces us to confront uncomfortable truths. When the righteous break rules in the name of justice, the line between hero and aggressor blurs. Victory may come but at a moral cost. Today, when people in positions of influence or authority choose ends over means—whether in politics, business, or personal lives—the erosion of ethical boundaries mirrors the final moments of the Kurukshetra war. Today, we see this when courts are misused to settle scores, or media trials are used to destroy credibility before facts are fully known, when journalists twist facts to win public trust, or when whistleblowers expose corruption using illegally obtained evidence. The cause may seem noble—but the means compromise the moral ground. Like the Kurukshetra battlefield, modern spaces of debate—courtrooms, boardrooms, even classrooms—wrestle with this dilemma: does purpose justify the breach?

Power without purpose, revenge masked as justice, and silence in the face of wrongs—these are not ancient dilemmas. They persist, dressed in modern clothes.

Ashwatthama's attack on innocent lives—on sleeping children and an unborn heir—was driven by vengeance, not valor. Today, we witness such blind retaliation in cyberbullying that targets families, smear campaigns that go after personal lives, or the sabotage of careers through anonymous tip-offs and internal politics. These are no longer battles of strength, but of strategy without conscience. Modern-day

Ashwatthamas no longer carry weapons. They launch silent attacks. They use information, leaked data, deepfakes to destroy reputations, often anonymously. Their actions aren't just impulsive—they're calculated, often irreversible, and meant to end legacies without leaving visible blood.

A student hacking into grades, a corporation hiding losses in accounting tricks, a charity flaunted for public applause rather than purpose—these are the modern reflections of war without ethics. Like Bhima, many justify breaking the rules because "the other side did it first." But what is lost in the process is deeper: the soul of righteousness. Each act chips away at a larger ethic—just as the final day of the war eroded the ideals that once held it together.

The Mahabharata does not offer a perfect ending. It offers a mirror—cracked and smudged, yet unflinching. The final day of war did not just kill warriors; it buried idealism.

When the thirst for victory outweighs the dignity of conduct, even dharma stands wounded. And sometimes, the deepest cuts are not made by weapons, but by intentions.

The Mahabharata doesn't end with a clean slate. Nor does life. It ends with a question: *what did we really win?* And if honour was broken on the way, can that victory ever truly satisfy?

Sometimes, truth doesn't scream. It doesn't always bleed. It just silently steps back, bruised—waiting for us to notice what we've lost.

CHAPTER 46

RENUNCIATION AND THE ILLUSION OF LIBERATION

Arjun's Final Doubt: Duty or Detachment?

As the war approached its devastating close, Arjun's confusion deepened—not about battle tactics, but about the meaning of duty itself. On the eighteenth day, surrounded by destruction and death, he turned once again to Krishna—not as a warrior, but as a seeker. His question was eternal: Should one withdraw from action in search of inner peace, or should one continue performing duties, regardless of inner turmoil, even amid chaos?

Krishna made a clear distinction between Tyaga (renunciation of the fruits of action) and Sannyasa (renunciation of action itself). He responded with clarity and depth: *Sannyasa* is the renunciation of action; *Tyaga* is the renunciation of attachment to the results of action. Neither, he explained, is spiritual in itself unless guided by the right intention. The essence of liberation lies not in giving up action, but in giving up the desire for reward.

Krishna was unambiguous—certain duties must never be abandoned. Acts such as sacrifice, charity, and austerity uphold the moral fabric of society. These are not optional, nor are they burdens if done without ego or expectation. True renunciation, he said, is performing one's role with discipline and detachment, not escaping from responsibility.

Even at the close of the Mahabharata, after having fulfilled his Kshatriya dharma and secured victory, Arjun remained burdened by doubt. His inner conflict mirrored the tragedy of the war—where behavior often lacked noble intent, and victories were laced with sorrow. The war had ended, but the battle within him had not. He stood as a symbol of a generation that won kingdoms but lost its moral compass, questioning whether their actions—however sanctioned—were ever truly righteous.

Three Types of Giving Up: What Krishna Teaches About Renunciation

In the Bhagavad Gita, Krishna explains that not all forms of "giving up" are equal. He describes three kinds of renunciation, based on three natural qualities (called *gunas*): Tamas, Rajas, and Sattva. Only one of them leads to true peace and freedom.

1. Tamasic Renunciation - Giving Up Out of Fear or Confusion

This kind of renunciation happens when a person avoids doing their duty because they are confused, lazy, scared, or don't want to face difficulty.

- **Why they give up:** Out of fear, laziness, or misunderstanding.
- **What happens:** They fall deeper into confusion and avoid growth.

2. Rajasic Renunciation – Giving Up for Personal Comfort or Gain

Here, a person gives up their responsibilities because they are painful or inconvenient, or because they want something better for themselves.

- **Why they give up:** For comfort, pride, or personal benefit.
- **What happens:** It increases selfishness and attachment to success or praise.

3. Sattvic Renunciation – Doing Your Duty Without Selfishness

This is the highest kind of renunciation. A person continues to do their duties, but without selfish desires or worrying about success or failure. They act with peace, wisdom, and a sense of responsibility.

- **Why they continue acting:** Out of a deep sense of duty and understanding.
- **What happens:** They grow spiritually and move closer to freedom and inner peace.

Krishna's Key Message:

True renunciation is not about stopping action or walking away from life.

It is about doing what must be done, but letting go of the desire for rewards.

He also says that no action is done by the person alone. Every action has five parts:

- the place,

- the person doing it,
- the tools used,
- the effort made, and
- the presence of the Divine.

To think "I alone am the doer" is an illusion.

So, the real path to peace is not in escape, but in selfless action. That is Sattvic renunciation—the only kind that leads to freedom.

The Inner Battlefield: Between Knowledge and Ignorance

Krishna warned that the ego-bound individual, who considers himself the sole doer, is trapped in delusion. Only the liberated—those who act without ego or craving—remain untouched, even when involved in the act of killing, as in Arjun's case. Their actions become tools of cosmic balance, not personal desire.

He further explained that knowledge itself varies by one's mode of nature:

- In **goodness**, knowledge is holistic and unifying.
- In **passion**, it is fragmented and self-serving.
- In **ignorance**, it is distorted, disconnected from reality.

Similarly, the intention behind action determines its moral weight. Actions done out of duty and detachment are noble. Those done for enjoyment or prestige are tainted. And those done blindly, violating ethics and conscience, are dangerous.

The Blueprint of Liberation: Self-Mastery, Not Escape

Krishna laid out the rigorous path to freedom: control over speech, moderation in food, withdrawal from sense pleasures, solitude, self-reflection, and abandonment of ego, desire, anger, and ownership. Liberation is not a gift but a disciplined inner conquest.

One who moves beyond like and dislike, who sees all beings with equanimity, who acts without seeking reward or recognition—such a person becomes eligible for the Supreme State.

The final counsel was clear: true renunciation is not an exit strategy—it's a mastery of being.

A Mirror to Today: Escapism Disguised as Renunciation

In today's world, many choices appear spiritual or wise on the surface—but often hide discomfort, burnout, or ego. Arjun's dilemma in the *Gita* finds striking reflections in our times.

- **The entrepreneur who sells everything to "live simply" in the mountains**—but refuses to face a failing business or broken relationships. This is not peace, but avoidance wearing the cloak of minimalism.
- **A high-achieving student who switches to a less demanding course**, claiming it's for "balance and well-being"—but deep down, it's

the fear of competition or a recent academic setback driving the choice.

- **The marriage that ends with one partner declaring "I've evolved spiritually beyond this relationship,"** when in fact, they're dodging personal responsibility.
- **The employee who suddenly resigns with a post about "prioritizing mental health,"** but the truth lies in unspoken workplace conflict or underperformance.
- **Influencers who delete their platforms claiming a need for 'digital detox,'** while quietly rebranding behind the scenes to escape public criticism, not ego renunciation.
- **A spiritual seeker who hops from retreat to retreat, avoiding a regular job or family duties,** claiming to "live in the now," while depending on others for basic needs.

These modern renunciations aren't always false—but when driven by ego, fear, shame, or convenience, they mirror Rajasic or Tamasic renunciation, not the Sattvic path Krishna honors.

Krishna's lesson wasn't about abandoning the world. It was about engaging with it meaningfully, without being enslaved by it. Renunciation, then, is not about *where* we live—but *how* we live. Not about *doing less,* but *desiring less*.

True renunciation doesn't run away—it remains engaged without being entangled.

CHAPTER 47

THE END OF MAHABHARAT: NOT THE END OF QUESTIONS

Yudhishthir's Rule: A Throne Built on Duty, Not Revenge

After the terrible war of Kurukshetra, Yudhishthir became the king of Hastinapur—not out of revenge, but out of a deep sense of duty. For 36 years, he ruled with fairness, kindness, and a strong commitment to dharma (righteousness).

He didn't let the pain of past insults or betrayals affect how he governed. Instead of holding grudges, he focused on healing a broken kingdom—rebuilding not just cities and roads, but also the trust and spirit of his people.

The real irony is this: Yudhishthir never wanted the crown out of greed or ambition. He accepted it out of empathy—for the people who needed peace, justice, and hope.It was not fueled by the fire of retribution but by the light of purpose. It is for this reason alone, as scriptures narrate, he alone among his brothers and Draupadi was granted entrance into heaven in his mortal body. The divinity of his desire transcended the bloodshed of the past.

The essence here is unmistakable: desire must be sanctified by duty. It must be directed by moral clarity, not clouded by emotional clutter. Yudhishthir's example stands as a timeless rebuttal to the assumption that desire and dharma are mutually exclusive.

Dhritarashtra's Blindness: A Metaphor Misunderstood

In stark contrast, Dhritarashtra—the blind king—lived a life of passivity and misplaced entitlement. His lament after the war, seated beside his grieving wife Gandhari, was not just about the loss of his hundred sons but of his own failure as a king, a father, and a man. Speaking to Sanjay, his faithful advisor, Dhritarashtra struggled to grasp how it all went so wrong.

But the truth was never out of reach. It was not his blindness that doomed him—it was his refusal to see. Physical blindness is not a barrier to ethical clarity or moral action. History is filled with individuals who, though deprived of sight, have led revolutions, inspired societies, and transformed nations. Dhritarashtra's true handicap was his willful inaction and emotional indulgence in his sons' wickedness.

He failed to understand that righteous action stems from insight, not eyesight. Sanjay reminded him of Krishna's teachings to Arjun—the Bhagavad Gita, rich in transcendental knowledge, action-oriented wisdom, and cosmic principles. Had Dhritarashtra internalized even a fraction of those lessons, he might have navigated his duties differently.

The Power of Words: When Speaking Becomes Doing

In the metaphysics of the Mahabharata, even sound is considered a form of action. Krishna's sermons were not mere philosophies; they were sound waves of energy and awakening. Modern physics too acknowledges the energy transmitted through sound.

Even today, science agrees that sound carries energy. The sacred sound "Om" is more than just a symbol; it represents a deep, creative force.

This reminds us of a bigger truth: action doesn't always have to be physical or dramatic. It can start with a thought, an intention, or even a single word.

King Dhritarashtra's silence wasn't just a political mistake—it had deeper consequences. His inaction created an energetic vacuum. By not speaking up or acting, he left an empty space—one that was quickly taken over by his sons' unchecked greed and ambition.

Why the Kingdom Fell: No One Taught Them Right from Wrong

Another reason for the fall of the kingdom was that Dhritarashtra didn't make sure his sons were raised with good values. He left their education to Dronacharya, a salaried teacher who lived in the comfort of the palace—not in the traditional forest-based gurukuls, where students learned discipline, simplicity, and strong moral values. As a result, the Kauravas grew up in luxury, without learning how to face challenges or develop inner strength.They were no longer tested by hardship; they were pampered by proximity.

In contrast, the Pandavas were raised by their mother Kunti, who taught them empathy, courage, and spiritual wisdom. Gandhari, though loyal and loving as a wife, didn't guide her sons in the same way. She gave birth to a hundred sons, but none of them were taught to be good, responsible people.

A ruler's duty is not just to protect the land—it is also to raise children, especially future leaders, who have strong morals and character.

Evil by Nature or Nurture?

Are villains born or made? The Mahabharata compels us to ask: is Duryodhana a product of an evil gene or a neglected moral education? Much like a snake, which when worshipped is holy, but when killed is justified—it is context, action, and intent that define good and evil.

Are bad people born bad, or do they become that way because they are not taught right from wrong? The Mahabharata makes us think about this question. Was Duryodhana evil by nature, or was it because no one gave him proper moral guidance?

Think of a snake—when it is worshipped, it is considered sacred. But if it is killed, people feel it was necessary. In both cases, the snake is the same. What changes is the situation and how people see it. In the same way, whether someone is good or bad depends on their actions, their reasons, and the situation.

A soldier who kills in war may seem cruel, but if he is doing his duty to protect, it is not considered wrong. On the other hand, a parent who fails to teach their child good values may not break any law—but their neglect can hurt society in the long run. Teaching children right from wrong is not just the job of parents, but also of leaders and elders. It must start from childhood.

Lessons from a River: Don't Rush Through Life

Nature teaches us powerful lessons—especially rivers. A river doesn't flow in a straight line. It meanders and slows down, and along the way, it leaves behind rich minerals. These minerals are like hidden treasures, mined only by those who stop and look carefully.

The lives of the Pandavas were also not straight or easy. They faced many struggles—exile, battles, and tough decisions. But they paused, reflected, and grew stronger. They learned from their experiences.

In contrast, the Kauravas rushed through life. They never stopped to think or question themselves. Their greed made them impatient, their pride made them blind, and their sense of entitlement led to their downfall.

The message is simple: if we rush toward success without self-awareness, we miss the wisdom that life quietly offers along the way.

A Lesson in Collapse: From Soil to Soul

In the Mahabharata, we often look at the grand events—wars, vows, miracles—but underneath it all lies a silent decay: the erosion of behaviour and noble intent. Was it a curse that destroyed the Kauravas, or was it their own deep-seated flaws that ensured their ruin? Like a tree with a diseased root system, no matter how tall it grows, collapse is inevitable. Botanists tell us that once the roots are infected, survival becomes uncertain.

Ancient ashrams were built deep in forests, away from the chaos of towns. They were sanctuaries for soul-searching, detached from the distractions of bodily desires. True knowledge arises when one can rise above the urges of the body. However, in our daily lives, we often fail to follow this vision. We indulge in actions that are clearly wrong, driven by delusion and unchecked desire. The fall of such a person is only a matter of time.

A Modern Reflection: Leadership in Crisis

Even today, we see the same pattern as Dhritarashtra's. Company leaders often say they didn't know their workers were being treated unfairly. Politicians act powerless while wrongdoings continue around them. Parents let their children do as they please but never teach them right from wrong. Instead of owning up to their role, people blame their actions on things like bad systems, bad luck, or just being unaware. Blame is always placed on "external forces"

But look at Helen Keller, blind and deaf, who became a global voice of courage. Or Sudha Chandran, who danced with a prosthetic leg. Or modern entrepreneurs from humble beginnings who now build social impact ventures. The limitation is never in the body; it is in the spirit.

Even in governance, the tragedy unfolds: when desire becomes self-serving rather than service-oriented, destruction is inevitable. We live in a time where leadership, much like in the Mahabharata, demands clarity of intent and alignment of action.

The Mahabharata's lesson here is stark and unforgiving. Dhritarashtra failed not because he could not see—but because he chose not to act. Yudhishthir triumphed not because he fought—but because he chose to serve.

In life, **vision is not about eyes—it is about insight.**

In leadership, **power is not about dominance—it is about purpose.**

And in character, **greatness is not about inheritance—it is about intent.**

To blame blindness for failure is to dishonor those who dared to lead in the dark.

CHAPTER 48

FROM MAHABHARATA TO MISSILES: HOW LITTLE WE'VE LEARNED

A Conflict Older Than the Mahabharata

The Kurukshetra war was not the first war of mankind, nor was it the last. Mythological accounts speak of cosmic wars in Patal (the netherworld) and Vayu Lok (the atmospheric realm), yet the Mahabharata war draws singular attention—perhaps because it unfolded on Earth, visibly, messily, and with lasting consequence. While it is tempting to see the Mahabharata as the beginning of war on land, archaeology tells a more layered story.

Geoscientists, anthropologists, and archaeologists have unearthed rich evidence that reveals human conflict predates the written word. In Epipaleolithic, Neolithic, and Chalcolithic times, mass graves, embalmed bodies pierced with obsidian shards, broken pottery, and primitive weapons litter the paleo surfaces of ancient lake margins. These relics do not just narrate the evolution of landforms; they scream of territorial fights, survival scuffles, and the aggression of early humans. These findings, although mute, show an instinctual readiness to fight, and the invention of weapons for defense and offense alike.

From caves, they observed. From observation, they learned. And from learning, they built the very tools of death. Early humans didn't try to understand life or seek truth—they just used their brains to hunt better, protect themselves, and make life easier. They used to make practical tools and solve everyday problems—things that were useful for survival. When early humans pulled back a bowstring, it sent the arrow flying. This could be seen as a symbol of how human anger turned into a targeted attack. Primitive cave paintings show both wonder and clever thinking. They are the first pictures of weapons like swords, spears, and slings.

The War Within the Family

The *Mahabharata* was not a war between enemy kingdoms. It was a war within a family—cousins turning into enemies, elders taking up arms against their own kin. It was a war that could have been avoided, but pride, ego, revenge, and greed for power led to destruction.

Even though the war was fought in the name of *dharma* (duty), it was driven by deeply human flaws. People blamed destiny, but the truth is that it was a result of choices—poor ones. It wasn't divine will, but a failure of human values that lit the fire of Kurukshetra.

Philosopher Thomas Hobbes once described it as "the war of all against all." That perfectly describes the Mahabharata, where no one truly won. No war has ever changed a victor's heart. In most cases, the winners become more arrogant and harsh. The real goal of war—if there ever was one—is often lost in the chaos and destruction it creates.

The war in the Mahabharata neither reformed society nor erased inequality. If anything, it justified vengeance, and glorified destruction as divine

Human Nature: Built to Create, Yet Prone to Destroy

Human beings have evolved over millions of years, carrying traits from earlier life forms —we can swim like fish, crawl like reptiles, jump like frogs, and walk like mammals. But it's not just our bodies; even our behavior has been shaped by evolution. The urge to survive, run from danger, fight, take control, or seek revenge—these instincts are deeply rooted in our brain and body.

Evolution gave us a brain capable of pausing, of reflecting, of choosing restraint over retribution. The tragedy of Mahabharata—and indeed of many wars before and after—was that this evolved capacity was sacrificed at the altar of ambition. The knowledge gained from observing nature never quite matured into noble intent. There's a painful contradiction in us: the same hands that can build tools, homes, and civilizations are also capable of causing harm and destruction. That gap—between our ability to create and our tendency to destroy—has defined much of human history, especially through the wars we fought and the stories we told.

War Is Not in Our Blood—It's in Our Mind

Some scholars have argued that war is in our biology—that we are wired to fight. They believe that war and violence are part of our biology. According to this idea, our anger and violent actions come from both outside reasons (like threats or competition) and inner drives (like aggression). Thinkers like Richard Dawkins linked aggression to our genes, saying we are naturally built for conflict. But many have challenged this idea. A more convincing explanation is that violence is learned through culture, upbringing, and environment.

Humans are not born with swords in their hands. We are shaped by our surroundings. History shows us that wars and revolutions often grow from social, political, and psychological issues—not just survival needs. In other words, people fight because they're taught to, or because systems make them feel they have no other choice.

Is war in our nature, or do we learn it? This question has always been raised

It is a matter of common observation that animals of the same species tend to live together in herds. They instinctively reject those different from themselves, often driving them away. Nature has equipped them with physical and instinctual mechanisms to protect their groups and retaliate when threatened. This instinct of retaliation fosters tendencies toward conflict and territorial defense. In this context, war can be seen as a biological necessity.

In prehistoric times, human beings shared a similar lifestyle. They hunted in groups and lived in caves, which necessitated the invention of weapons—both for protection and for hunting. Conflicts with other groups over territory or shelter were frequent, and thus, fighting became essential for survival. War, in this sense, evolved as a need deeply linked with biology, emerging culture, and rational faculties.

Wars have historically stemmed from various causes, such as aggression, resource control, power dynamics, and ideological differences. Numerous literary works have explored war from different philosophical and psychological perspectives. Understandably, as technology advanced, the concept of war also evolved.

Stories Shape Memory, Not Always Truth

Much of what we know about early wars comes from stories passed down by word of mouth. These oral traditions were later written down, often changed or exaggerated to match the storyteller's view. That's why many ancient war stories don't give us the full picture of what really happened—they reflect emotions, ideals, or warnings, not accurate records.

When writing was invented, these stories were written down. But they were often changed or made more dramatic, based on how people remembered them or wanted them to be remembered. They were often distorted or romanticized—based on the collective memory of many generations. So, many early written records may not tell us exactly what happened in history—they tell us how people *felt* about it or what they *believed*

From cave drawings to epic poems, humans have always tried to explain and justify war. But with each telling, the line between truth and myth becomes blurry.

From Gurus to Guns: How Teaching Lost Its Soul

Character-building begins at home. Parents are a child's first teachers, helping them learn love, discipline, and values. In ancient India, this task was later passed on to the *kulguru*—a family teacher responsible for both education and character.

In the times of the *Ramayana* and *Mahabharat*, teachers like Dronacharya trained princes in both knowledge and warfare. These gurus advised kings, and even fought in wars. They were deeply respected.

But over time, the role of the teacher changed. Some gurus became selfish, stopped accepting traditional offerings, and misused their students for personal gain. This decline showed in the moral fall of those they taught.

A good teacher understands each student's needs and helps them grow. But even the best teacher can't help a student who refuses to learn. Arjuna succeeded because he was humble, focused, and eager to learn—unlike others driven by arrogance.

Modern War: New Tools, Same Mindset

Today's wars look different, but the mindset behind them hasn't changed. Instead of bows and chariots, we now have nuclear weapons and drones. Instead of battlefields, we have boardrooms and political stages. But the desire to dominate, control, and eliminate competition remains.

Nations stockpile weapons not just for defense, but to show power. Satellite images replace cave drawings, but the goal remains the same: control territory, inspire fear, and assert dominance.

Even in cities, corporate rivalry resembles war. Strategies are made not to build together, but to destroy competitors. "Development" projects often displace poor communities—these are silent battles with real victims.

We may dress up these conflicts with polite words, but underneath, the primitive instinct to overpower others still drives many of our actions.

When Evolution Lacks Ethics

We have come a long way in science and technology—but our wisdom has not kept pace. The *Mahabharata* reminds us that without values and ethics, progress means little. We've moved from caves to skyscrapers, from arrows to missiles—but we're still stuck in old ways of thinking.

If we don't grow in compassion, wisdom, and restraint, every new invention becomes a sharper weapon, not a better tool. We're still hunting, still fighting—only now with more dangerous toys.

Wisdom Must Outpace Weaponry

Until we learn to choose peace over pride, dialogue over domination, and humility over ego, we will repeat history—again and again.

The real victory lies not in defeating others, but in overcoming the need to fight.

Relevance in the Modern Day

Modern boardrooms, political stages, and digital battlefields may seem far removed from ancient caves or chariot wars, but human behavior hasn't changed much. The drive to dominate, compete, and win—regardless of cost—still shapes our world.

Take, for example, the global arms race. We no longer throw spears or shoot arrows; we now build nuclear weapons, cyber armies, and AI-guided drones. The cave drawings have been replaced by satellite imagery, But the goal remains the same: to intimidate, to claim power, and to protect self-interest.

In the corporate world, business takeovers and market battles often reflect cold wars in disguise. Corporations may not use weapons, but they use strategy to eliminate rivals, sometimes putting profit above ethics, sustainability, or human welfare.

Even urban development projects—often called symbols of progress—can result in the forced displacement of thousands. Entire communities are uprooted to make space for highways, malls, or tech parks. These are not traditional wars, but they still create casualties—loss of homes, culture, and dignity.

The tools have changed, but the thinking hasn't. We continue to evolve technologically, but without ethical growth, our progress remains hollow.

Evolution Without Ethics Is Regression

The Mahabharata reminds us that evolution without ethics is merely aggression in finer clothing. Humanity may have journeyed from caves to condos, from bows to ballistic missiles, but without noble intent guiding action, we remain what we began—hunters by instinct, not guardians by choice.

Until wisdom matures faster than weapons, every war—ancient or modern—will be a monument to our moral failure.

Until wisdom develops faster than weapons, every war—ancient or modern—will be a monument to our moral failure.

EPILOGUE

As the final page turns, what lingers is not just the memory of epic battles, divine interventions, or ancient oaths—it is the echo of a question that refuses to fade: Have we truly learned from our past? The Mahabharata, written thousands of years ago, is not merely a tale of cousins at war; it is a profound reflection on the human psyche—our pride, greed, loyalty, and dharma. Each war cry and whispered prayer in its verses mirrors our modern dilemmas: political ambition, moral compromise, fractured families, and broken promises.

This book attempted to hold a mirror—not to the world outside—but to the one within. By drawing parallels between ancient warfare and today's conflicts, between characters of yore and leaders of now, it becomes clear: while our weapons have evolved, our instincts remain alarmingly the same. Arjun's hesitation on the battlefield is every human's inner conflict between duty and desire, ethics and ambition. Krishna's cosmic vision is not a spectacle but a reminder: that truth, though eternal, must be chosen consciously in every age.

MESSAGE TO THE READER

Today, wars are no longer started with swords, but with satellites and signed documents. Yet, the Mahabharata reminds us that the most important battles still happen inside the human heart. No matter how advanced we become, without wisdom, restraint, and compassion, we are bound to repeat history in deadlier forms.

Let this book be not just a reflection but a call—to rise above pettiness, to understand our roles in the larger cosmic play, and to choose righteousness even when it hurts. The Mahabharata does not ask us to be perfect; it asks us to be aware.

May we not wait for destruction to remind us of truth.

Let dharma be our guiding force—before the conch is blown, before the first missile is launched.